LOVE, SEX AND NO REGRETS

FOR TODAY'S TEENS

Advance praise for *Love, Sex and No Regrets For Today's Teens*

'For some time I have been documenting girls' experiences with porn-saturated boys. Girls relate cold, soulless hook-ups which leave them feeling hurt and used, of sexual bullying and harassment, of not knowing how to say 'no', of putting up with sex acts they don't welcome or enjoy, of feeling like sexual service stations for boys, of emotional disconnection in scenarios where intimacy, tenderness and authentic human connection play no part. Reading *Love, Sex and No Regrets*, it seemed the author had spoken to the same girls.

'Elizabeth Clarke describes fast, unpleasant, unsatisfying, disconnected sex which offers nothing "artful, masterful or even sweet and tender." Elizabeth describes sex as "a huge part of our spiritual world, our desire for connection, our search for meaning and purpose."
This long overdue and refreshingly real book will help girls fight back against pornography's indoctrination, to recognise that bad sexual experiences injure their bodies and minds, to stand up for themselves, to avoid boys who are cruel sexually and socially, and to be empowered and self-caring enough to put their minds, bodies and spirits above impersonal, detached and meaningless sexual transactions. In short, to see that sex is, in Elizabeth's own words, *too intimate to compromise*.'
– **Melinda Tankard Reist**, author of *Big Porn Inc*, speaker, advocate for women and girls, and co-founder of Collective Shout

'Elizabeth Clark is the very best sex educator in the world. Her writing on this subject knows no peer.'
– **Steve Biddulph**, bestselling author of *Raising Boys* and *Steve Biddulph's Raising Girls*

'This is the book I wish I had when I was a teen. Entertaining, honest, informative and empowering, [it] demystifies love, sex and everything in between.'
– **Daria Snadowsky**, author of *Anatomy of a Boyfriend*

LOVE, SEX AND NO REGRETS
FOR TODAY'S TEENS

ELIZABETH CLARK

FINCH PUBLISHING
SYDNEY

Love, Sex and No Regrets For Today's Teens

First published in 2017 in Australia and New Zealand by Finch Publishing Pty Limited, ABN 49 057 285 248, 64 Darley Street, Mona Vale, NSW, 2103, Australia.

17   8 7 6 5 4 3 2 1

Copyright © 2017 Elizabeth Clark

The author asserts her moral rights in this work throughout the world without waiver. All rights reserved. No part of this publication may be reproduced, stored in a retrieval system or transmitted in any form or by any means (electronic or mechanical, through reprography, digital transmission, recording or otherwise) without the prior written permission of the publisher.

ISBN:9781925048889

There is a National Library of Australia Cataloguing-in-Publication entry available at the National Library.

Edited by Megan English
Cover and internal typeset by Jo Hunt
Printed by Griffin Press

Reproduction and Communication for educational purposes
The Australian Copyright Act 1968 (the Act) allows a maximum of one chapter or 10% of the pages of this work, whichever is the greater, to be reproduced and/or communicated by any educational institution for its educational purposes provided that the educational institution (or the body that administers it) has given a remuneration notice to Copyright Agency Limited (CAL) under the Act. For details of the CAL licence for educational institutions contact: info@copyright.com.au

The paper used to produce this book is a natural, recyclable product made from wood grown in sustainable plantation forests. The manufacturing processes conform to the environmental regulations in the country of origin.

Finch titles can be viewed and purchased at **www.finch.com.au**

CONTENTS

FOREWORD	VII
PROLOGUE	IX

PART 1 KNOW WHAT'S POSSIBLE	XIII
ONE OH, MY GOD	1
TWO CLICKING THE SWITCH	9
THREE MINDFUL SEX	14
FOUR CONNECTION	19
FIVE THE BIG O	23

PART 2 KNOW THE BASES	27
SIX PORN HAS NO BASES	29
SEVEN THE BATTER'S BOX	34
EIGHT FIRST BASE	40
NINE SECOND BASE	44
TEN THIRD BASE	49
ELEVEN HOME RUN	53
TWELVE KNOW THE NO	57

PART 3 KNOW THE REST 63

THIRTEEN **FLIRTING** 65
FOURTEEN **VIRGINITY IS NOT A BACKPACK** 70
FIFTEEN **EXERCISE IN SELF-PLEASURE** 73
SIXTEEN **CYBER-SEXUAL CONNECTION** 77
SEVENTEEN **CONNECT AND DISCONNECT** 83
EIGHTEEN **SAFE SEX** 87
NINTEEN **SEXUAL ASSAULT** 94
TWENTY **ACCEPT ONLY THE BEST, LADIES** 97
TWENTY-ONE **DUDES** 101
TWENTY-TWO **LET'S DO IT** 104

POSTSCRIPT 106

FOREWORD BY STEVE BIDDULPH

I first came across *Love, Sex and No Regrets* in a little hand-printed edition, all the way from the Rocky Mountains of Colorado. And it knocked my socks off. It was funny, sexy and wise, and it had an approach to love that was so affirming and joyful, in a world that is mostly full of danger and misuse.

And oddly, it was the answer to that world. A kind of compass/radar/inner wisdom that could get a young person right to where the good stuff is, while avoiding the bad. And without any of the embarrassing stuff, which they know anyway.

The best thing about the book is that while it is purportedly aimed at teens, it is actually an advanced guide to love for anyone of any age.

The problem we have in the world today is not that there is too much sex in our faces everywhere, but that it's not really sex at all, it's just – I don't know – lost people getting more lost. Sad and empty humping and pumping … like getting the most amazing ice cream in the whole world and trying to shove it in through your belly button, instead of actually tasting it.

Young love is so awesomely wonderful when it's done right, with vulnerable openness, and shy exploration, talking and absolute full attention to the here and now. And, well, you know what I mean. We get a glimpse of heaven, and we are happy for the rest of our lives to make that journey back.

In a world that says either 'get her done' or 'don't do it', *Love, Sex and No Regrets* is the voice of a mysterious desert witch, warrior woman, goddess godmother saying 'do it well!' Do it slow. Do it the way you choose, by listening to your inner voice. Build the fire. Test the waters. Set the bar high. Take some risks, but don't settle for less than everything right. Get your heart and your mind and your body all lined up and see what a storm that can make.

I was training a group of advanced therapists in the year when I discovered this book. They were the best twelve therapists in the state, women mostly, and far more worldly wise than me. I bought multiple copies and asked them all to read it. They grinned so broadly when they returned my copies, I almost wasn't game to ask what they thought. But I did, and they all said 'Yes!'

STEVE BIDDULPH
(who was young once and really, still is)
Adjunct Professor of Psychology, author of *Raising Boys*, Steve Biddulph's *Raising Girls* and *The New Manhood*

PROLOGUE

The microphone waits patiently to amplify my voice. I'm nervous because I'm about to give the valedictorian speech at my high school graduation – and I'm pretty sure I'm going to offend some adults; maybe all of them.

'Hello!' I say enthusiastically.

'Hello!' the crowd cheers back. I like the feeling.

'It's our time!' I yell to my classmates. My fellow graduates scream and shout.

'We need to thank all our family members, teachers and administrators for their love and support,' I say like every other top student at every other high school graduation across the globe. I mean it, but while I'm saying the words I wonder if I have the guts to say the rest. I think I do, but I better warm them up a little more.

'You've given us so much. So much of your time and energy, your hope, your forgiveness.' I pause. The audience chuckles. 'Your concern and, of course, your wisdom.' The smiles and applause are soft and sweet. 'And we needed you so much because we face futures that will require the best of us. We will need strong bodies. We will need strong minds. We will need strong hearts.'

They clap politely.

Here goes.

'If you are proud of your graduate, STAND UP!' I demand.

The entire crowd bounces to their feet clapping and cheering.

'Stay standing for a moment,' I say. And then I act like I'm just coming up with this idea, 'You know, there's one thing I think we missed here in high school.'

The crowd waits for me to make my point, certain I will be amusing.

'I think you could have given us wisdom in one area that would have helped us out a lot.'

They grow a little restless waiting for what they are sure will be some more praise.

'So, I have a little experiment.'

Silence.

Then I say it. 'Sit down if you've never seen porn.'

The stunned crowd remains standing.

'Sit down if you waited until marriage to have sex.'

A very few people sit.

'So please sit down if you did not know how to honestly –'

I pause.

'Respectfully –'

I pause again.

'Courageously …'

I take a breath.

'… help your children navigate their sexuality.'

They hesitate. I see the principal's eyes pop out as he stands up and starts heading towards me. Still, I wait them out. This is important. Then, in a sort of wavy unison, the nicely dressed audience sits.

'I don't know if you realised most of our sex education came from porn stars, not you. We've been on our own, drowning in the cyber-sexual world.'

The principal comes up from behind me and grabs my arm. I hold tight and look to my friends, my class, then shout: 'Let's change the course of our futures. Let's alter history. Let's have amazing sex lives!'

A bunch of stuff happens at once. The microphone gets shut off. The now-seated crowd grumbles. The principal escorts me off the stage. My parents decide to return the new car they got me for my graduation. The attending school board member considers withholding my diploma. The journalist from the local paper wakes up with a wicked smile and begins writing like mad.

The only important thing that happens is that my classmates begin to wake up from their sexual slumber. My words ooze into their minds doped with memories of confusing, disappointing, shameful, embarrassing, heart-breaking – and sometimes physically harmful – sexual experiences.

A kid I know stands, points at me and yells, 'Hannah!'

A few more stand and start to cheer, then ten, twenty. Big chunks of my gown-clad peers rise. Soon every single kid is on their feet cheering, hands high above their heads. The last image I see as I am led out of the stadium is my graduating class climbing onto their chairs, cheering.

I know they don't quite know why they are cheering. They just know there is a slight breeze of hope for our future. They don't know exactly that it is a future where soft, slow kisses satisfy way more than some porn-inspired hook-up; a future where we can discover great sex lives.

xii LOVE, SEX AND NO REGRETS

They just know something true is in the air.

Don't worry about me, though. While I do drive a second-hand Corolla, I still got a full scholarship to my third-choice university. It was worth it.

PART ONE
KNOW THE POSSIBILITIES

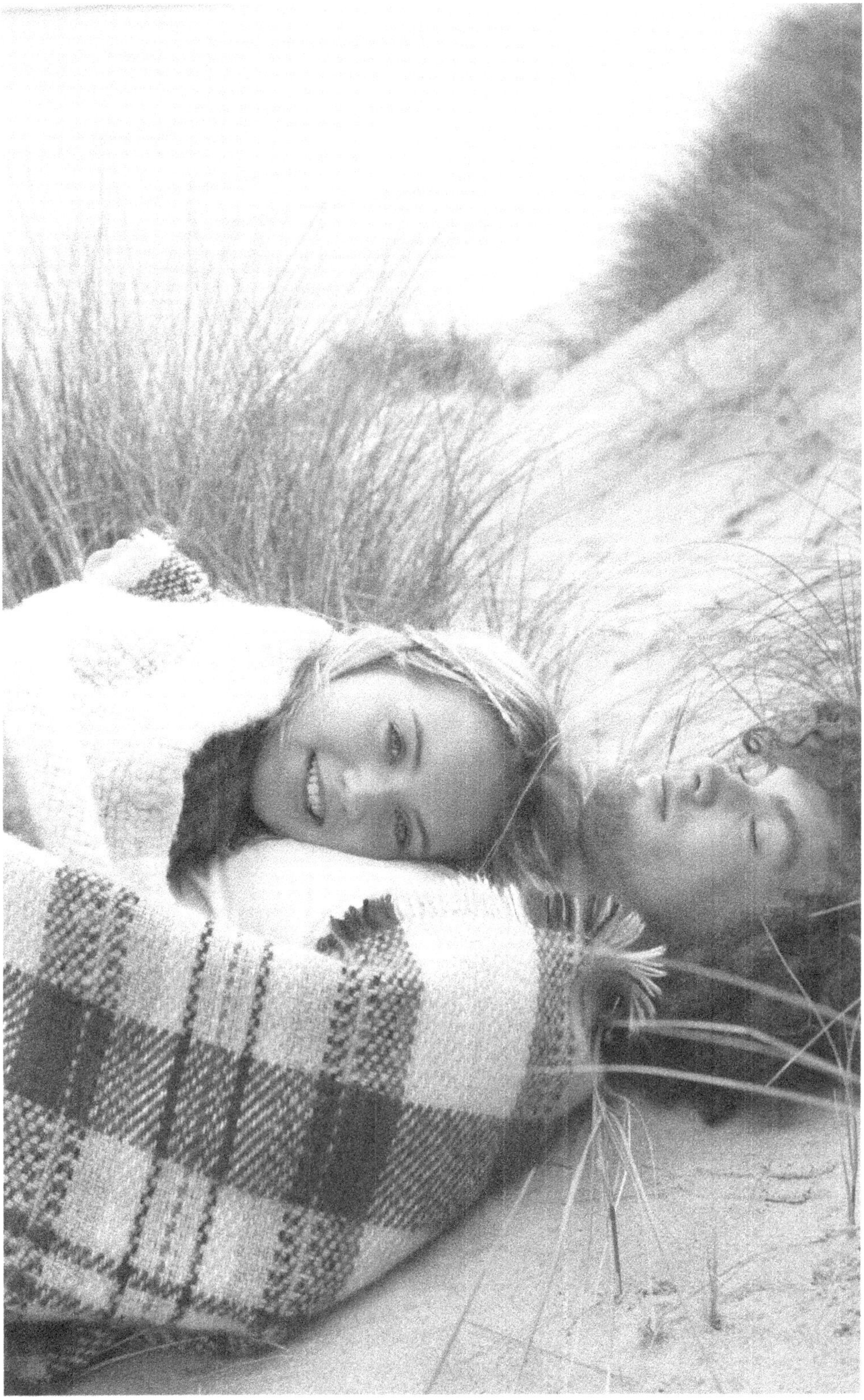

ONE
OH MY GOD

Sex.

Yeah ... sex.

Let's declare a revolution on sex. Now. Big time. Let's proclaim we will have great, amazing, fun, powerful, oh-my-god sex lives.

Let's do it differently than those before us.

Let's banish shame.

Let's banish guilt.

Let's banish insecurity.

Let's banish fear.

Let's really banish ignorance, especially the misinformation we've learned from internet porn.

Let's learn from those who studied and mastered sex not just for pleasure, but for its ability to empower, to connect, to heal, to evoke awe, to open creativity, and to zoom us straight to the heavens.

Let's picture a future where we no longer act like nine-year-olds hiding our eyes when the prince kisses the girl. Let's not deny our healthy sexuality and in doing so open the gates of hell to the porn model of sex, sexual abuses and passionless futures that lead to crazy divorce rates.

LET'S NOT DENY OUR HEALTHY SEXUALITY.

Yep, I blame all of this on ignorant and misinformed views of sexuality.

Why am I writing this book? Because I can and I will. I'm Hannah Dugan, age nineteen. I was the top student of my high school. I was the editor of my national award-winning high school newspaper, senior class president, and president of the National Honour Society. I was offered full scholarships to the top ten universities.

I come from a good and loving family. We went to church every Sunday and Wednesday night. Until my senior year, I'd only kissed one boy – badly.

My family clearly believes sex is for marriage and sexuality is to be put away until the wedding night. Oh, you can dress sexy as hell for the Year 10 and Year 12 formals, just 'don't be slutty'. You shouldn't engage in sexy talk or have lingering sexy thoughts until 'the night'. After the vows and wedding cake, only then can you do *it*. Then you have a few kids and do it less and less.

I'd already decided that teen sex was no fun, especially for girls. Too many of my friends told me about the sex they'd had and it sounded horrible. It sounded fast – insanely fast – and unpleasant. And unsatisfying. To make things worse, it seemed that as soon as it went from making out for about a minute to having sex, the boys turned into emotional zombies who got as far away from the girls as possible. That was definitely not going to happen to me.

Anyway, last summer I fell in love with a boy named Joe. Love! We only had a few weeks together, but in that time my body and soul woke up!

Joe was this confident, beautiful boy who loved me, loved himself and loved our bodies and our souls.

Holding hands with Joe was sexier, more erotic, more arousing than most teen sex I'd heard about. Hell, it was sexier than *any* sex I'd heard about. We stared into each other's eyes. We kissed. God, did we kiss. We made out and our bodies tingled with an energy I didn't even know existed. We did a bunch of other stuff, too.

I wanted to do it all. ALL. My body didn't care about religion, or marriage, or anything. I wanted sex. Really wanted sex. Wanted Joe. All of him.

One night Joe smiled breathlessly between kisses after we'd walked all over town, making out at every secluded spot we could. This included picnic tables at the park, up against some trees, and on the dew-moistened grass by the lake. His hands were running up and down my back. I felt his whole body pulse. I had just said, 'I want to have sex with you.'

'Oh Hannah.' His mouth went against mine, tongue finding mine.

Then he pulled back and stared into my eyes. His smile was amazing. His desire was amazing.

I was so excited and terrified. I said to myself, *'I'm gonna have sex. This is it. This is the moment.'*

'It's not tonight,' he said as his hands pulled up my shirt so he could touch the skin of my back. His hands stopped just at the top of my jeans.

'It's not going to be me,' he continued. 'Not us.'

I knew in an instant he was right. I knew we weren't ready. I didn't really care because what was happening to my body under the zipper of my jeans was like nothing I'd ever experienced before. All I wanted to do was have him touch me there. I didn't care with what.

I KNEW IN AN INSTANT HE WAS RIGHT. I KNEW WE WEREN'T READY.

I knew that sex wasn't going to happen that night, but I was crazy with want, with desire for release. Joe rolled me over on my back and pressed his full weight on me. As he kissed me, he tilted himself against me. I tilted myself hard against him. Our mouths made this perfect circuit.

And then it happened.

I exploded. All that built-up want was released in an explosion. I had an orgasm. I moaned and arched my back. I knew things at that moment. I knew I wasn't separate from anyone, anything. I knew my perfect worth and the perfect and equal worth of everyone. I realised I wasn't my looks, my family, my money, my grades … my resume. I knew Joe and I were one and we soared to the cosmos somewhere. That huge pulsing took me to a place I'd only experienced a few times before in my life, but never like this. Never this rocket to joy. This was perfect and huge.

Oh My God!

I didn't even try and contain my pleasure over this experience. I moaned and ground myself against Joe.

Then it began to fade. I quickly left the heavens and returned to my body under Joe's.

I was amazed and exposed. I was quickly not excited or aroused any longer. I felt incredibly close to Joe. I loved him so much.

He smiled at me. He was so happy, so dear. He rolled off me, which I appreciated because I was relaxed. So done.

I knew he wasn't, but he wasn't angry or demanding more. I could see he was breathing deeply, pulling away from his passion and his desire for release.

I loved this man. Loved him.

'I can't believe what just happened,' I said.

He smiled. 'Amazing.'

'Joe, this is something.'

'Yes.'

'I love you.'

'I love me, too,' he laughed, then said seriously, 'Hannah, we love each other.'

I could have felt stupid and exposed, but I was with Joe. I felt loved and peaceful. But more than all that, I felt like I'd discovered something no-one had ever told me about. Like I had a million dollars in a bank account I could access any time. I realised that sex isn't some dirty thing, some sin, something to do only to have kids.

Sex isn't the hump. It isn't the frantic, empty stuff you see on TV. It isn't what happens at parties where everyone is drunk. It isn't something we do to prove our worth, our social status or our sexual orientation. It definitely is not – or at least should not be – what porn models for us.

I realised sex is a huge gift from whatever creative force built this life of ours. Sex is a huge part of our spiritual world, our desire for connection, our search for meaning and purpose. Besides all that, it is so normal and natural, like breathing and smiling.

SEX IS A HUGE GIFT FROM WHATEVER CREATIVE FORCE BUILT THIS LIFE OF OURS.

I'd just figured out that sex is a glorious gift and I, Hannah, was going to find out everything about it. I was going to discover why no-one had ever told me about it. I was going to uncover why most teen sex was so bad, so not what I just experienced.

I'm smart. I write well. I research like a mad woman.

I interviewed teens and adults about their sex lives – not just about intercourse (crappy word!), but about their entire romantic and sexual lives. I asked about great sex and bad sex. I asked about relationships. I asked about orgasms (great word!). I got my brother, Jo Sha (a.k.a. Joshua), to interview guys because it got too awkward when I tried.

I looked up articles on healthy, happy sexuality and found entirely different ways of looking at sex. I found ancient teachings that saw sexuality as a sacred art form. They transformed my entire view on sex. They gave me hope for our future.

I'm not a slut. I'm not a whore. I have simply become an expert on teen sexuality and on the ancient teachings on the art of sex.

I'M NOT A SLUT. I'M NOT A WHORE. I HAVE SIMPLY BECOME AN EXPERT ON TEEN SEXUALITY AND ON THE ANCIENT TEACHINGS ON THE ART OF SEX.

I am committed to our generations creating a better life than the one being handed us.

Why sex?

Because I believe it is a driving force for change. I also believe it has been a driving force for oppression, making us feel bad about ourselves, making us fear our bodies and desires. I believe older, more advanced cultures studied and mastered sexuality. They left us directions, like treasure maps. I think the landscape has changed, but we can find it, and then use it in our way, in our time.

I believe what I said in my speech: we do face difficult challenges. We need to be as healthy and creative and self-confident as possible. We need great sex lives.

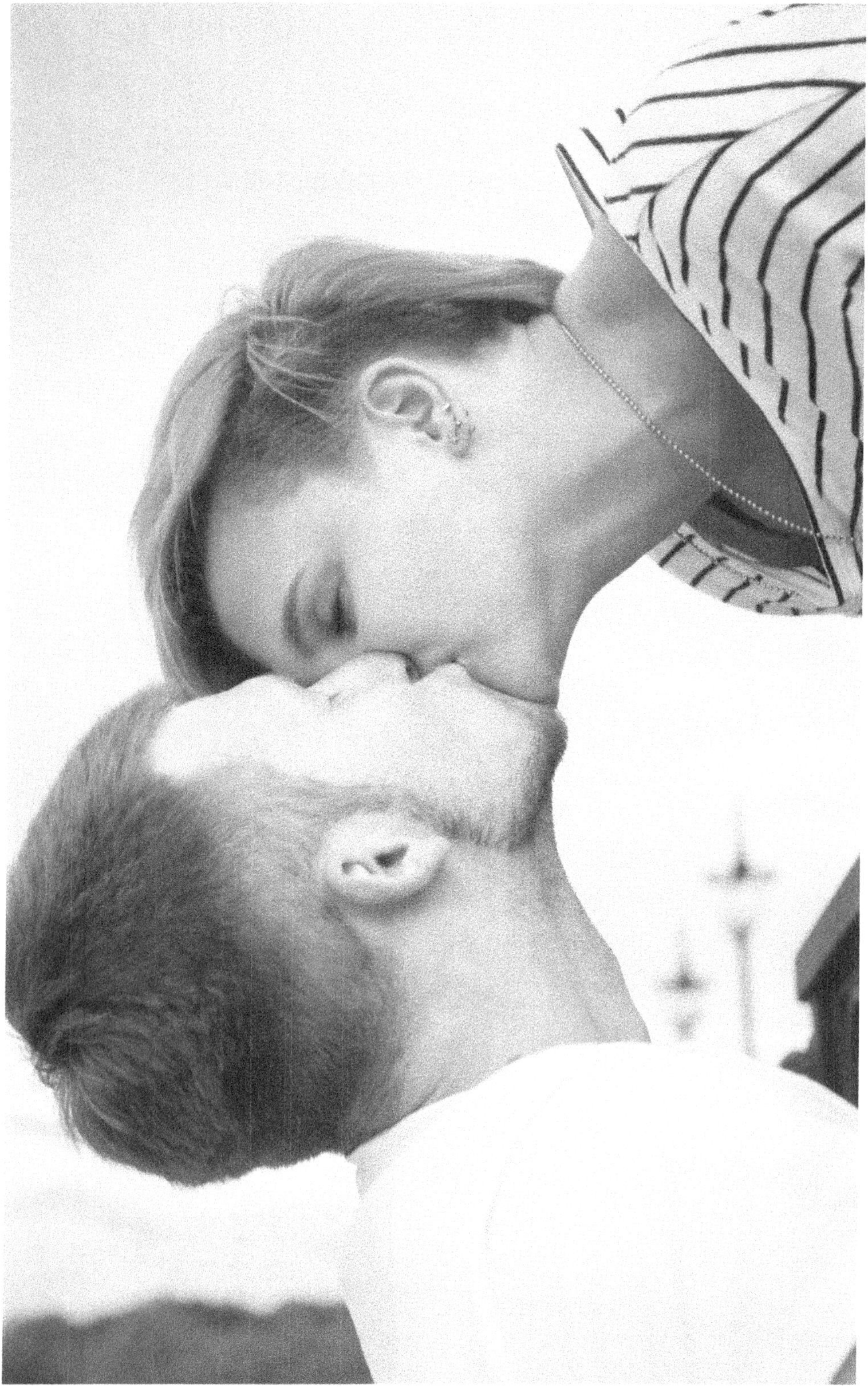

# TWO
CLICKING THE SWITCH

Remember when kissing on TV made you sick? When any member of the opposite sex made you sick? When you first learned about doing *it* made you sick? When everything you learned about doing *it* made you sick? Remember?

Remember when some older kid, or later, some friend suddenly got interested in *it*? Talked about *it*? Did something like hold hands, kiss or make out? Remember how kids loved to tell stories about all sorts of kids doing all sorts of things including *it*?

Remember how *it* scared you, grossed you out, and angered you because of how wrong *it* was?

Maybe you're still there, but if you are reading this, your switch has probably already clicked, or at least it is twitching.

You went from horrified to curious. From a body that went cold at such thoughts to a body that grew warm with such thoughts, that squirmed with such thoughts. A body that could stop concentrating on school or family or friends or anything in order to ponder all the aspects of *it*, of romance, of sexuality, of sex itself.

This happens at different times for different kids. Some kids are young when their switch clicks, some are pretty old. Some switches click huge and some stay rather mild. Regardless, the switch does click, and in one of a zillion ways you go from sexually asleep to wide awake. You go from thinking there's no way you'll ever do anything as disgusting as *it* to someone who is pretty sure you will.

SOME KIDS ARE YOUNG WHEN THEIR SWITCH CLICKS, SOME ARE PRETTY OLD.

Know this: every adult's switch clicked on at one time or another. Just like yours did. Adults and kids often forget this.

Now, the clicking of the sexual switch should be an amazing time, but it is often a time of great conflict and pain. It didn't used to be that way. Not so far back in history when we hit this age of switch clicking, we married. We married young in perfect timing with our bodies.

We married at the ages of fifteen to nineteen, right when our bodies were dying to have sex. But we began to postpone the appropriate age of marriage so that we'd be older and better parents, better educated, better financially prepared to start families. And we postponed and we postponed. Now the average age of marriage in our culture is thirty-one for men and twenty-nine for women.

So, here we have these bodies designed by God himself with switches clicked full on, and we're supposed to wait and wait for five, ten, fifteen years?

Tension mounts. Rules are made. Adults who have obviously

forgotten all this make more and more rules. They tell us to put our sexuality out of our minds (like they did!), they tell us to abstain (like they did!), but they give us no alternatives. Nothing.

Our sex education consists only of the medical mechanics of sex, the possible horrid consequences of sex (like STDs and unwanted pregnancies), and lectures on waiting. Sex education is usually taught right alongside drug education, like it's something bad. No wonder we're all messed up about it.

Look at the pathetic state of teen sex education in our culture. We have huge abstinence messages *and* huge pornography influence. Sex is everywhere – every ad, our clothes, movies (even PG), TV (with naked tops and bottoms, and full-on sex) and the mother-of-all-porn-dispensers, the internet.

So adults are screaming, 'Don't do it, but swim in it while you wait.'

Well, guess what? Our sex, our generation's sex, sucks. Because we're mostly using porn to show us how sex is done, we're having some of the least evolved, interesting, mature, loving or spiritual sex ever. I know this because I asked.

OUR SEX, OUR GENERATION'S SEX, SUCKS ... WE'RE HAVING SOME OF THE LEAST EVOLVED, INTERESTING, MATURE, LOVING OR SPIRITUAL SEX EVER.

According to teens I interviewed, our sex is fast, uncreative and unsatisfying. Yet many teens are certainly having sex. Eighty per cent of us will have sex before we are twenty – 80 per cent. That's a lot more than most of us. So we are having sex. We're having bad sex, and no-one is giving us honest advice. No-one is giving us true wisdom – wisdom that admits that sex is a strong and potentially great force in every human's life.

Where are the answers to the real questions we have? Like, what is good sex like? How do girls have orgasms? How do you know your body is ready for sex? How do you know if you're ready for sex? How do you feel connected sexually? How do you go from kissing to intercourse? (What a horrid word!) How do you not feel stupid afterwards? How do you honour your body and its desires *and* honour your parents and beliefs?

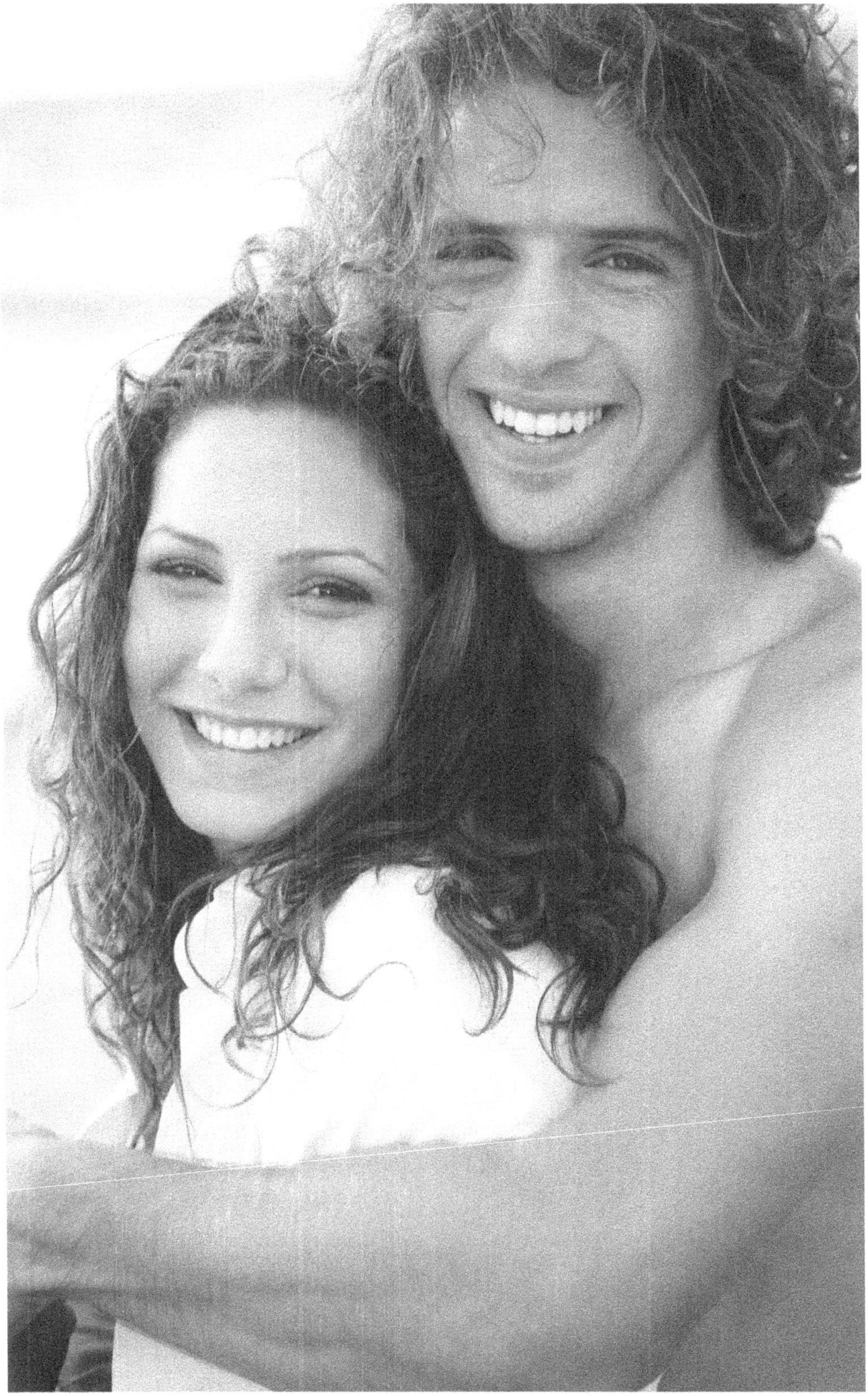

THREE
MINDFUL SEX

Mindful sex is sexuality that isn't just something a body does without thought (like burping or picking your nose), but something you master like playing an instrument or making an amazing meal. Older civilisations had schools of thought that taught people how to transform mindless sexuality into an art form. They called them the sacred sexual arts. *Tantric Sex* and *The Kama Sutra* are the best known, most published, and easiest to access.

MINDFUL SEX IS ... SOMETHING YOU MASTER.

They all say basically the same thing: sex is a sacred art.

Think about that. First, sex is sacred. Why? Is it? Most of the stories I hear about actual intercourse don't seem too sacred.

What does sacred mean anyway? My dictionary says it means 'declared holy'. Declared holy? Right up there with church, communion, Christmas and baptism? Aren't they all declared holy?

How can fumbling around in the back seat of your car be holy?

How can a drunken make-out session be holy? How can sex modelled after porn sex be holy?

Holy: 'associated with divine power.'

Divine power.

When most people hear the words *power* and *sex* together they think of whips and chains, but really, sexuality itself – mastered – produces power. At least that's what other cultures believe. In fact, in the ancient civilisations of India, Japan and China, the sexual arts were considered secrets known only by royalty, the wealthy and the powerful. They didn't want the servants or common people knowing them. They needed a class of powerless people.

Powerless people. How sexy are they?

So can you become powerful through sexuality? Oh yeah. There is an old movie you probably never saw called *The Matrix*. The premise is that artificial-intelligence machines have taken over the world and they use our bodies as batteries to keep themselves charged because we really are all copper-tops that produce and store energy. We can be cheap batteries that run out of juice quickly or long-lasting rechargables.

To be fully charged, we need great circuitry that flows without obstacles. This circuitry needs to be flowing well inside us so it can flow to and from others. Things like nature, beauty, inspired thoughts, laughter, creativity, joy and love help a lot. Flow and recharging can certainly come from mastered sexuality.

Yet that isn't the kind of sexuality teens are experiencing. I hear kids talk about sex like it was something they own and collect. Kind of like 'I *got* to go to Hawaii', 'I got so high last night', and 'I got these really cute jeans', or 'I *got* laid'.

16 LOVE, SEX AND NO REGRETS

Got.

Huh. There is no flow in *got*.

But if someone talks about what came before *got*, what they say does seem holy, not *got*.

Attraction. Eyes met. Shy smiles exchanged. Talk about nothing while bodies talk, decide. Move closer. Touch, lean into, shove a little, tickle and wrestle. See the best in the other, that person of desire. Connect. Eyes, then maybe hands. Arm around shoulder, around waist. Lean into. Eyes. Smiles. Lick of the lips. Body wide awake. Eyes.

That beginning, the things you say, the way you think, the kindness, the tenderness, the fun, the play, the connections and, most important, the way you see the dazzling worth in the other and in yourself. That, my friend, is holy.

THE THINGS YOU SAY, THE WAY YOU THINK, THE KINDNESS, THE TENDERNESS, THE FUN, THE PLAY, THE CONNECTIONS AND, MOST IMPORTANT, THE WAY YOU SEE THE DAZZLING WORTH IN THE OTHER AND IN YOURSELF. THAT, MY FRIEND, IS HOLY.

From here we don't seem to know where to go. So we go from holy to *got* and lose the wonder. It is in the space between holy and *got* that so much pain occurs in relationships.

But, it doesn't have to be that way.

The sacred sexual arts teach ways of mastering one's sexuality to eliminate the pain that occurs between holy and got.

That's the art form.

Tantric texts speak of the Sixty-Four Sacred Arts – everyday art forms, many of which are free or very inexpensive, and don't need years of formal instruction. They include singing, reading, music, writing, drawing, painting, sewing, dancing, poetry, sports, pottery, gymnastics, games, flower arranging, cooking, decorating, gardening, languages, etiquette, carpentry, magic, chemistry, minerology, architecture, religious rites, household management (I love this one!), disguise, martial arts and about thirty-five others.

Tantric teaching believes if you bring some of these into your life, you will be enriched with beauty, peace, harmony, joy, connectedness, generosity and great balance. You'll be fully charged and your energy will flow well. According to the texts, sex is the only art form we must *all* study. We may choose from the rest.

What a different way of thinking about sex. Revolutionary, really. To think of sex as something to be studied, practised and mastered. This involves patience, focus and alertness. Otherwise it's just squeaking out notes on a violin like first-year players do in middle school. It's fun enough, but not beautiful – and you certainly don't start off playing duets!

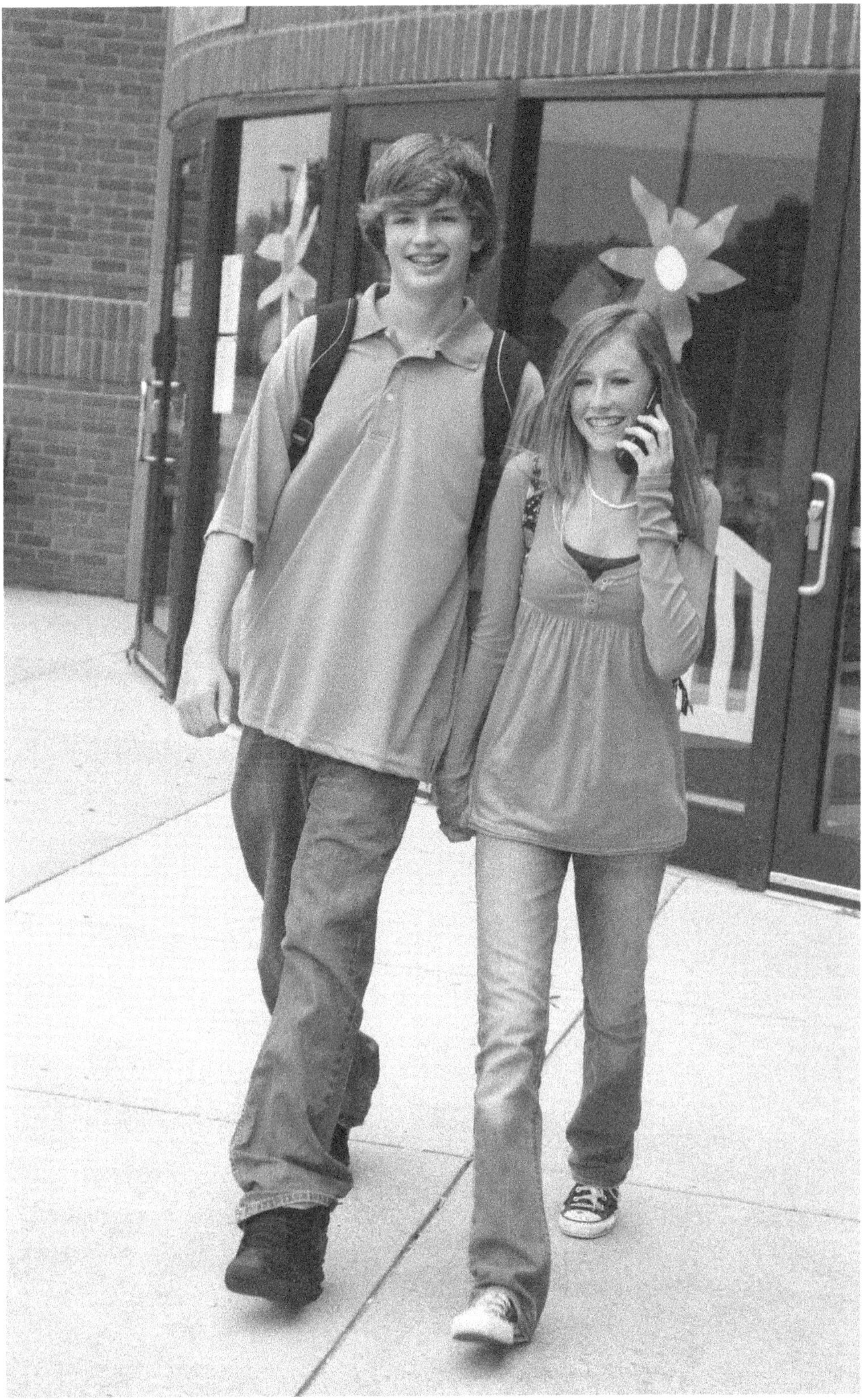

FOUR
CONNECTION

If sex is an art from, then connection is the medium. Connection becomes the watercolours to paint with, the notes to play, and the ink to create the words.

It's all about connection.

My favorite greeting goes like this: put your hands together over your heart and bow slightly. The other person does the same. They you say, 'Namaste' (pronounced nah-ma-stay), to one another. It means, loosely translated, 'the divine in me acknowledges the divine in you'.

Can you imagine what our sex lives would be like if before each embrace, each kiss, each sexual act along the way to sex, we acknowledged the divine in the other.

Talk about connection.

It may sound corny and unrealistic, but isn't that what the first moments of attraction are all about? Aren't we seeing the best, the divine in the other? Aren't we really saying, 'The best in me acknowledges the best in you?' or 'The soul in me sees the soul in you?' Or, 'The sexy beast in me acknowledges the sexy beast in you?'

Sometimes when I'm racing through the halls at school I make myself stop and watch everyone. I look at the blank faces trying to pretend they don't need connection, when in fact we are thirsty for connection; for divine connection. If I happen to catch someone's eyes I smile a smile that tells them I see their worth. It's magic. They light up.

WE ARE THIRSTY FOR CONNECTION; FOR DIVINE CONNECTION.

I think we're standing in a river of connection, yet we're dying of thirst. There are all these glorious souls we can connect with, but we just pass them by, not knowing we could drink. Not knowing we never have to be thirsty again. Never alone.

Our habit is to disconnect. We are quick to gossip, hate, fear, and create drama and chaos. We get distracted by our huge want of everything. We would rather be entertained than connected.

All we have to do is stop and see the divine worth in ourselves and the other.

Then we can paint!

Mary Pipher writes in her book *Writing to Change the World*, 'If I have one great idea, it is that connecting people might save the world.' That is a great idea! How we connect sexually is a huge part of how we connect in general. Isn't sex one of the ultimate connections?

What the hell is connection anyway?

This gets back to the fact that we are all energy. And energy can only move, can only be powerful, through connection. That is why we have to plug the computer into the electrical sockets. That's why wires hang across our towns and under our cities. Electricity moves from source to source.

A great visual for this are Plasma Globess. Sometimes you can find them in science stores or those shops that sell T-shirts we aren't allowed to wear at school. They're like glass globes of electrical currents. If you touch them, the current finds your hand. It seeks you out. It doesn't hurt, but you can feel it through the glass. I own one of these and touch it all the time, just to remind me of what's happening between all of us, all the time – only we can't see it.

Imagine. Every minute we're sending out those tentacles of electricity, like little lightning bolts. Then, when we're near others, we connect electrically. The closer we get, the greater the potential for connection.

Not all connection is warm and fuzzy and sexy. We all know this, that's why we choose not to connect.

The main forms of connection are either weak and dull connections (boring), the ones where we try and take the energy of others or they try and take our energy (yuck!), or the kind where together our joined energy creates bigger and greater energy (amazing!). We plug into the huge energy that moves the oceans and created both the cosmos *and us.*

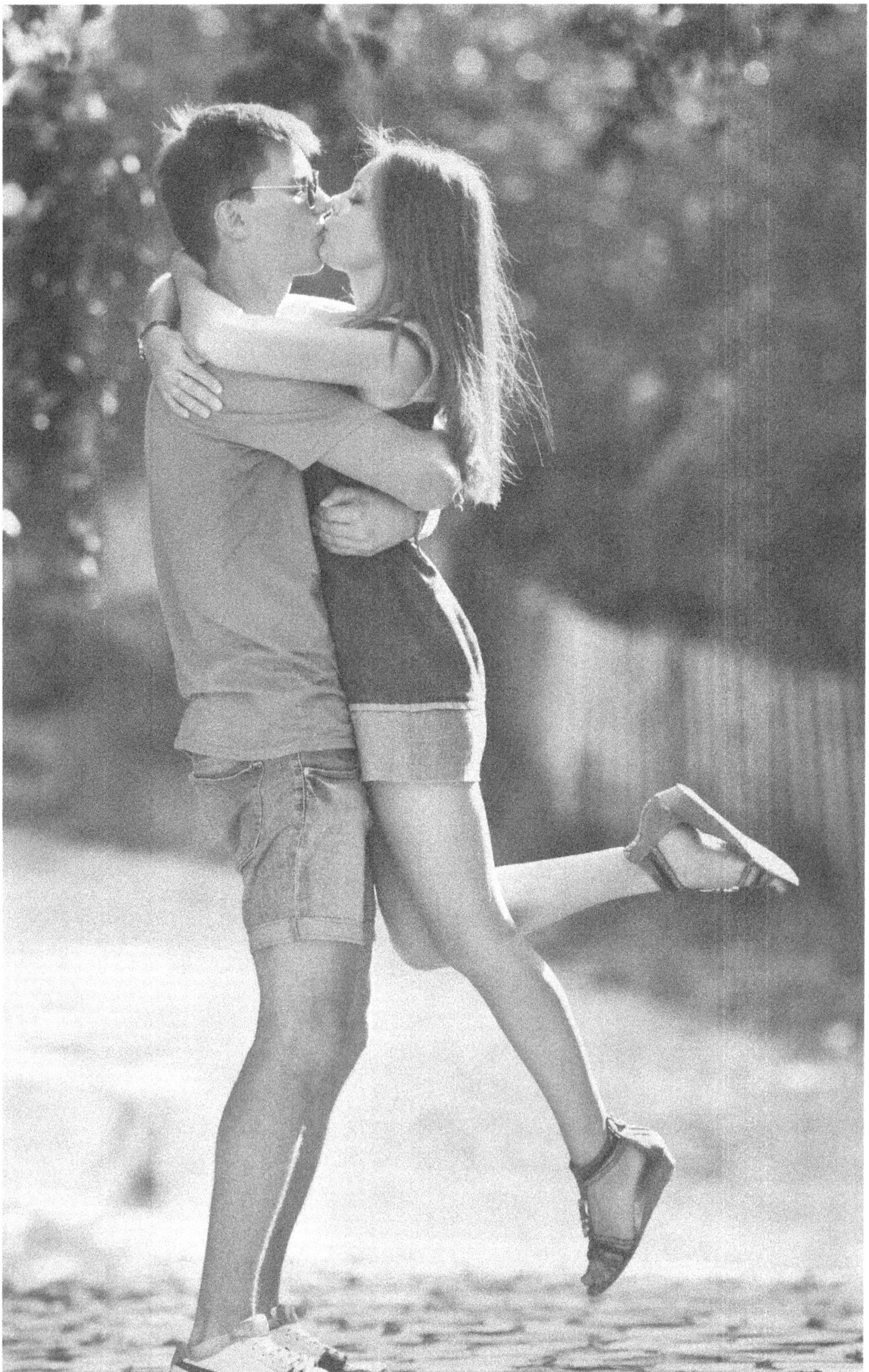

FIVE
THE BIG O

This brings us to the Big O, the Big Bang. Yep, the orgasm.

Enlightened adults may say, 'Orgasm is not the primary goal of sex,' but come on, it is certainly the hope of sex.

Or *release*, as it is called in the sacred arts.

Release after great build-up.

I love the term orgasm. It is the only sexual term that is beautiful and perfectly descriptive. It sounds just like what occurs during an orgasm. You build and build and build with tension and excitement. You expand and expand. You go beyond the confines of your body. Our internal circuitry begins firing at an incredible rate. And though the energy starts in your groin, it radiates out through your torso to your fingertips and from your thighs to your feet. (There are brain-imaging videos of what happens in the brain during an orgasm.)

In tantric sex, orgasm is used as a way to begin mastering your sexuality.

First and foremost, you don't learn about orgasm from someone else. You learn it from yourself.

Most kids I interviewed reported that once their 'switch clicked', they thought they should immediately go have sex. Many did. Most said the experience was a let-down because the goal was simply to have sex, to de-virginise, to find out what it was all about. There was nothing artful, masterful or even sweet and tender. They just did *it*.

Having sex soon after your switch has clicked is like trying to play a solo at Carnegie Hall right after you get your first violin. It's gonna be bad – really bad.

We don't learn to have sex by having sex. A lot of kids and adults who have had bad early sexual experiences said that although they've had some okay sex later, overall they didn't think sex was all that great. They seemed eternally disappointed by it.

We learn about good sex by exploring our own sexuality. We learn sex by studying sex, not the lies in porn! We learn about sex by knowing ourselves. Don't let anyone but you teach you about your body. You could end up feeling resentful, disappointed, embarrassed and alone. These are not the feelings sex is supposed to bring!

WE LEARN ABOUT GOOD SEX BY EXPLORING OUR OWN SEXUALITY.

I am fairly certain if Joe and I had had sex that night it wouldn't have been good. Up until then, I didn't know my body or sexuality at all. Now I do. Now I'm an expert on myself.

So first, know thyself.

Yes, I'm talking about masturbation (but will use the term *self-pleasure* from now on). I think it is a nicer word.

It's pretty clear that most boys can self-pleasure, but they might not know there are many ways to self-pleasure. (I believe this the beginning of bad future sex. With porn as a major model for sex, speed and disconnection becomes the habit. We'll go into this more later but for now, boys, consider self-pleasure as the groundwork for future great sex.)

Self-pleasure for girls is more complicated. In my interviews I found that girls don't want to talk about this topic. It seems some girls self-pleasure, but plenty don't. Some didn't even know what I was talking about. Some had tried but with no luck; no orgasm. Many thought the idea was too embarrassing and gross to even try. (Interesting. I thought having sex with some random guy you met an hour ago was truly embarrassing and gross.)

Doctors will tell you (even though you probably won't ask), that there are health benefits to self-pleasure – it provides a healthy outlet for people who choose to abstain, allows people to get to know their sexual bodies, reduces stress, helps you sleep, and encourages self-esteem. So there.

And while religions and belief systems differ widely on sex, sexuality and self-pleasure, very few even discuss orgasm. It seems to be the where and with whom and when that gets regulated.

It is a good idea to know your beliefs and make decisions from there about self-pleasure.

Should you decide practising self-pleasure is a way to master sexuality, there is an exercise in Chapter 15. (Can you believe it?)

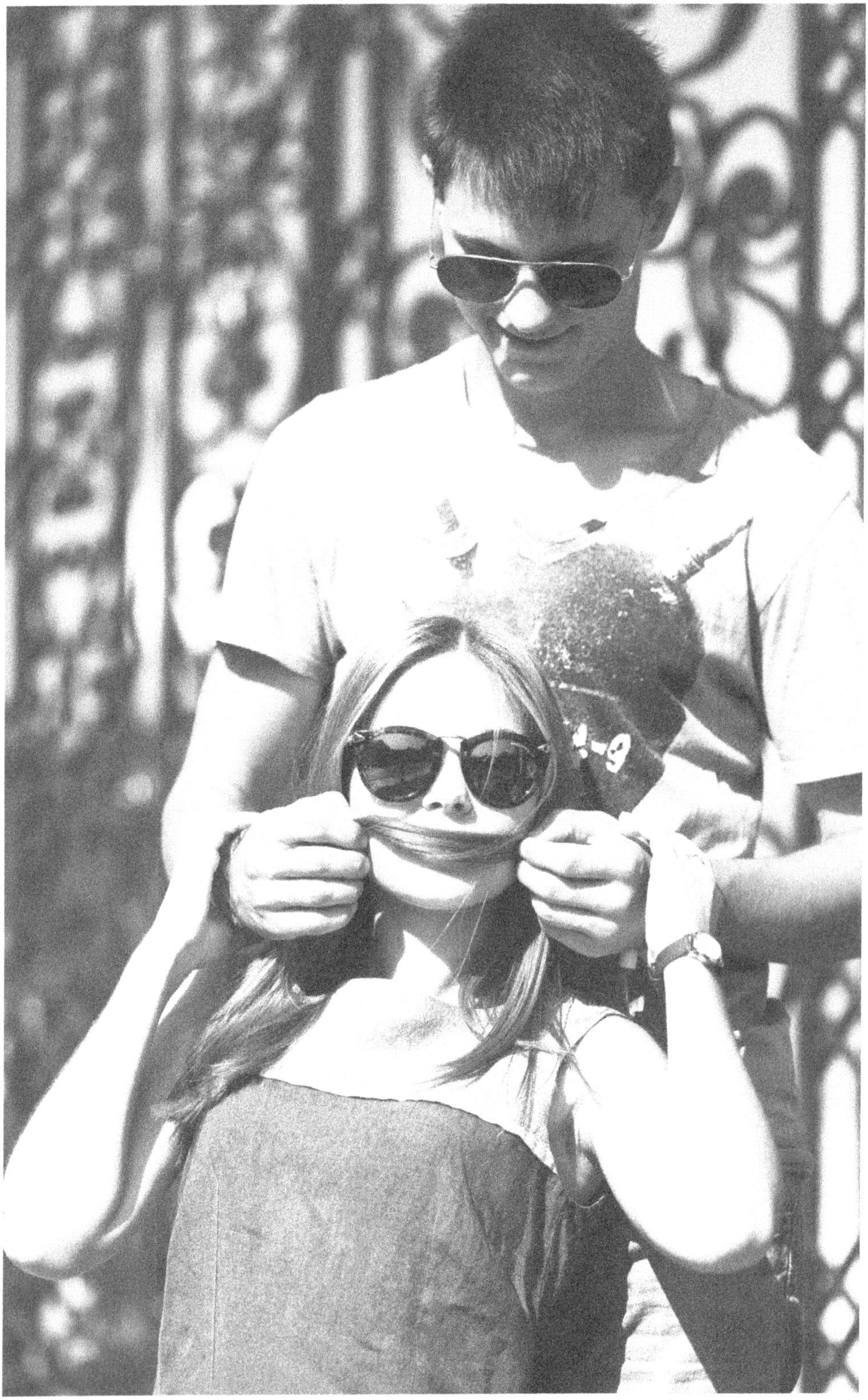

PART TWO
KNOW THE BASES

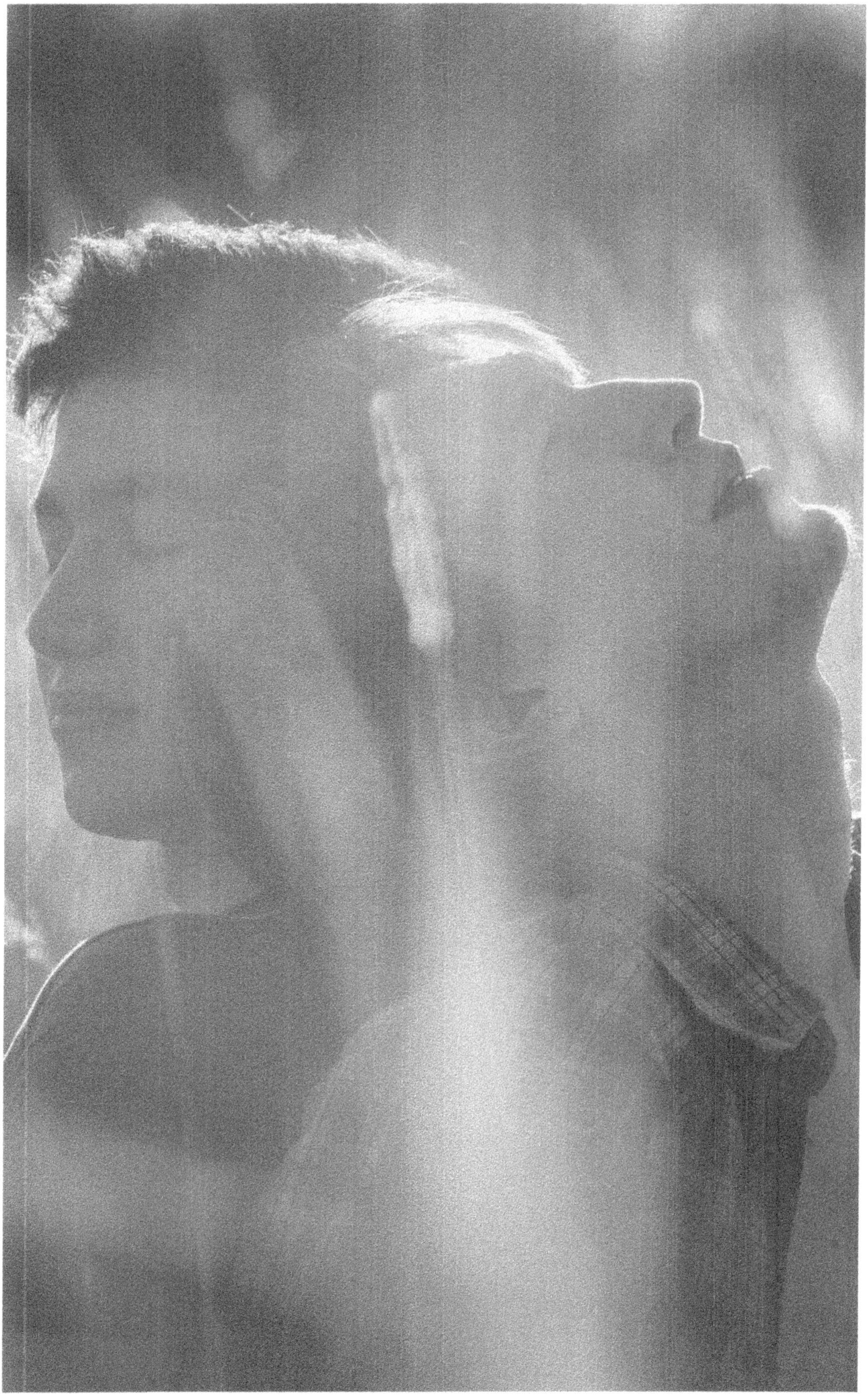

SIX
PORN HAS NO BASES

I love baseball. I love the smell of the dirt. I love the sound of the bat cracking after a perfectly hit ball. I love the taste of roasted peanuts. I love the pace of the game because it's all about how you get from here to there.

So I have decided to use the standard baseball metaphor – first base, second base, third base and, of course, the home run – to describe the steps taken on the path to sex. Ancient tantric teachers would roll in their graves if they thought I was reducing all the steps required down to four. I'm not. I am simply categorising them into the four: attraction, touching, intimate touching and sex.

Unfortunately porn, not baseball, became our model for sexuality when our parents handed us our phones, computers and tablets. They didn't mean to. They just didn't know. They didn't understand how messed up our sex lives would become. They thought they were handing us the world. And they were – they just didn't factor in that porn is a fairly big part of that world.

UNFORTUNATELY PORN, NOT BASEBALL, BECAME OUR MODEL FOR SEXUALITY WHEN OUR PARENTS HANDED US OUR PHONES, COMPUTERS AND TABLETS.

We are the first generation whose sex lives have been so influenced by internet porn. Most of us have seen it. It was the first image of sex that most of us had. Porn has become our most powerful teacher about sex.

This is a problem because *porn sexuality is nothing like good sexuality*. Watching porn as kids just learning about sex is like toddlers watching slasher movies learning about love. It has messed us up. And even if you weren't influenced by porn, the chances are your partners were.

So let's re-educate ourselves. There was no evil conspiracy. Porn was never meant to teach us. Porn was created to turn people on so they could self-pleasure. That's it. It's sort of weird and fast and intense so people can have orgasms all by themselves. Both boys and girls I interviewed said the images of porn terrified them when they pictured themselves having that kind of sex. Even though it did, indeed, turn them on.

LET'S RE-EDUCATE OURSELVES.

So here are the simple lies taught by porn.

1. Anybody will do as a sex partner.
2. From the minute two people (or way more!) show some sign of attraction, sex happens immediately. There are no bases.
3. As soon as sex begins, it is important to have zero emotional connection. Eye contact, caressing, saying nice things are not encouraged.
4. The rhythm of sex is a constant and hard pounding. That is what works.
5. People (mostly women) love to be injured and degraded during sex. Love it.
6. After whatever has happened during the sexual encounter, everyone is happy. Everyone had a great time.

Right. So here are the truths about real sex.

1. We're not really attracted to everyone. It does matter who you chose to be sexual with. Our bodies do care. Some people, many people, in fact most people just don't do it for us.
2. Bodies take time to get aroused. There are many very nice and fun steps from a kiss to sex that should not be skipped. Sex without arousal is like well, sex without arousal. It leads to bad sex and there are not many worse experiences than bad sex.

3. Emotional connection is important. After random, disconnected, hook-up sex most partners experience depression. Orgasms happen far less in emotionally disconnected sex. (Yes, even for the men.)
4. Pounding is not the best model for sex. Good sexuality is creative and varied in its intensity, timing and motion.
5. No-one likes to be injured. When your body or sense of worth is being injured during sex, let's just be honest: that kind of sex sucks. You can even experience depression and PTSD symptoms. The fantasy of some of these things can turn us on, but the reality usually leaves both partners feeling traumatised. What starts off as consensual sex can be experienced as sexual assault.
6. No-one had a good time. No matter what they say. No matter how much we try and tell ourselves how great it was because the porn stars certainly seemed to be happy doing the same things, no-one had a good time.

EMOTIONAL CONNECTION IS IMPORTANT.

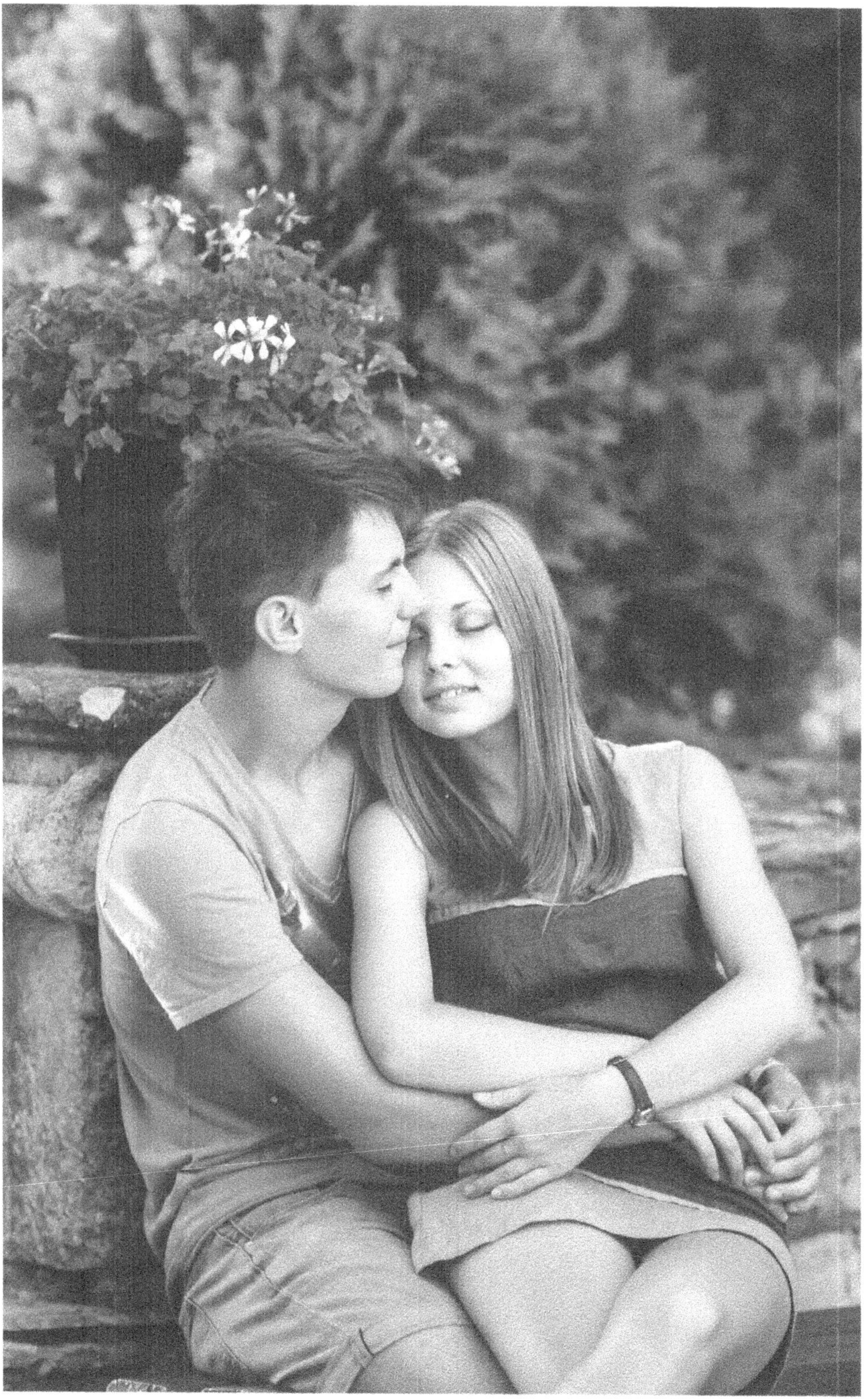

SEVEN
THE BATTER'S BOX

In real life – not a porn-inspired life – there are hundreds of amazing steps from attraction to sex. The first step is to simply know your beliefs. If you think any sexuality should not be explored until you are of a certain age, not living in your parent's house, married or with someone who has the same beliefs as you then stop right here. Beliefs are important. Breaking our beliefs is harmful. Honour them. Guilt and shame are not the ingredients to great sex lives.

But when you know you are about to start your romantic and sexual life, be aware that there are lots of steps along the way, and each step requires a decision.

* 'This isn't what I thought. I want to get out of this situation.'
* 'This is fantastic. I want to stay here.'
* 'This is too far. I want to go back a step.'
* 'This is too fast. I want to stop.'
* 'This is amazing. I want to go to the next step.'

✱ Or, in our porn-inspired sexual world: 'This is okay, maybe we should skip sixty steps and have sex.' Ugh!

If you believe what most teens say and what the sacred sexual texts say, the main reason our sex lives are marginal is because we don't take our time. We skip most of the steps. Hell, we don't even know there are steps let alone the possibility of a great sex life! And we don't allow ourselves the time to connect emotionally and energetically.

All sacred sex teachings emphasise that the body is perfectly created for sexuality. Our bodies unfold to sex. There is a process, a natural progression that leads to great sex.

So if you're thinking about heading to home plate and facing the pitcher, or if you want to get in the game, you need to know the bases and you need to be prepared.

THE BATTER'S BOX: KNOW YOUR WORTH

If you don't know much about baseball, the batter's box is the area near home plate where the next batter stands and practises their swing while watching how the hitter on home plate is doing.

I added the Batter's Box because tantric teaching emphasises that before you begin your romantic and sexual life with others, you must first prepare yourself. And learning about your own sexual body is part of that preparation. Even more importantly, if you're going to have a good sex life you have to know your own worth. (Actually, I'm guessing that if you're going to have a good life of any kind you need to know your own worth.)

IF YOU'RE GOING TO HAVE A GOOD SEX LIFE YOU HAVE TO KNOW YOUR OWN WORTH.

When we were young, like before we were six or seven, we never, ever thought about our worth. We knew we were worthy. Hang out with any little kid and you will be reminded of this – they never, ever worry about their worth. They know they *are* worthy.

Then we were taught that our worth is not our beating hearts and our perfect uniqueness. We were taught that our worth is our wealth, beauty, family, possessions, successes, jobs, friends, education, grades and sexiness – or lack thereof.

But we used to know the truth. We knew our worth was as constant as the warmth of the sun, the spin of the earth and the wag of our dogs' tails. We knew our worth is absolutely equal to everyone else's.

Brain scans show that people who do not pair their worth with the everyday ups and downs, the failures and successes, with their possessions, their number of *friends* or *likes*, with each kilogram on or off, each dollar in their wallet are significantly happier, accomplish more and, I will add, much sexier. They spend far less energy proving, defending and protecting their worth.

There is an oddly easy way to get back to knowing your worth is constant and not something you must prove and defend. For one month say, 'Doesn't change my worth' for every thought you have about yourself. 'I look great … doesn't change my worth.' 'I bombed that math test … doesn't change my worth.' 'I am nervous/sad/depressed/embarrassed/heartbroken/furious/joyful … but it doesn't change my worth.' The next month, whenever you have a strong feeling, judgment or comparison about someone say, 'Doesn't change their worth.' You might worry this will turn you into a self-centered slug. It won't. It will give you tons of awesome energy.

Since you are in the batter's box and all full of worth (or on your way and reminding yourself as often as needed), there are some other things you might want to improve before you get in the game. These are great habits to practise whether you're playing ball or not. When it comes to sexuality, we usually focus on our bodies.

The tantric teachings go over specific ways of living that enhance our self-confidence and therefore, enhance our sexuality.

Simple things.

Hygiene. Brush your teeth, your tongue, and floss. (I added that one. They didn't have floss back when these texts were written.) Wash, well, everywhere ... every crevice. Wear clean clothes. Smell good without having to wear a gallon of cologne like SAW or Eau de Pop Star.

Get outside. Walk. Go into nature. Get some sun (safely), some exercise. We feel sexier when we've been near beauty, near wonder.

Laugh, especially with others. Laughing is sexy. Really. Laughing is a way to remember how connected we are, which reminds us of our worth. Laugh.

Creativity is sexy.

Eat well. Fast food, salty food, fatty food and sugary foods are not sexy. Cook and eat meals. Eat more veggies and fruits. Have dinner with your family and friends. Healthy skin, hair and bodies are sexy.

Stop watching TV and playing video games all day. (I added this one, too.) They turn you into slugs. Slugs are not sexy. (Unless you are a slug.)

That's it. These things might not seem too sexy on their own, but when you add them together, you're ready to play ball. Batter up!

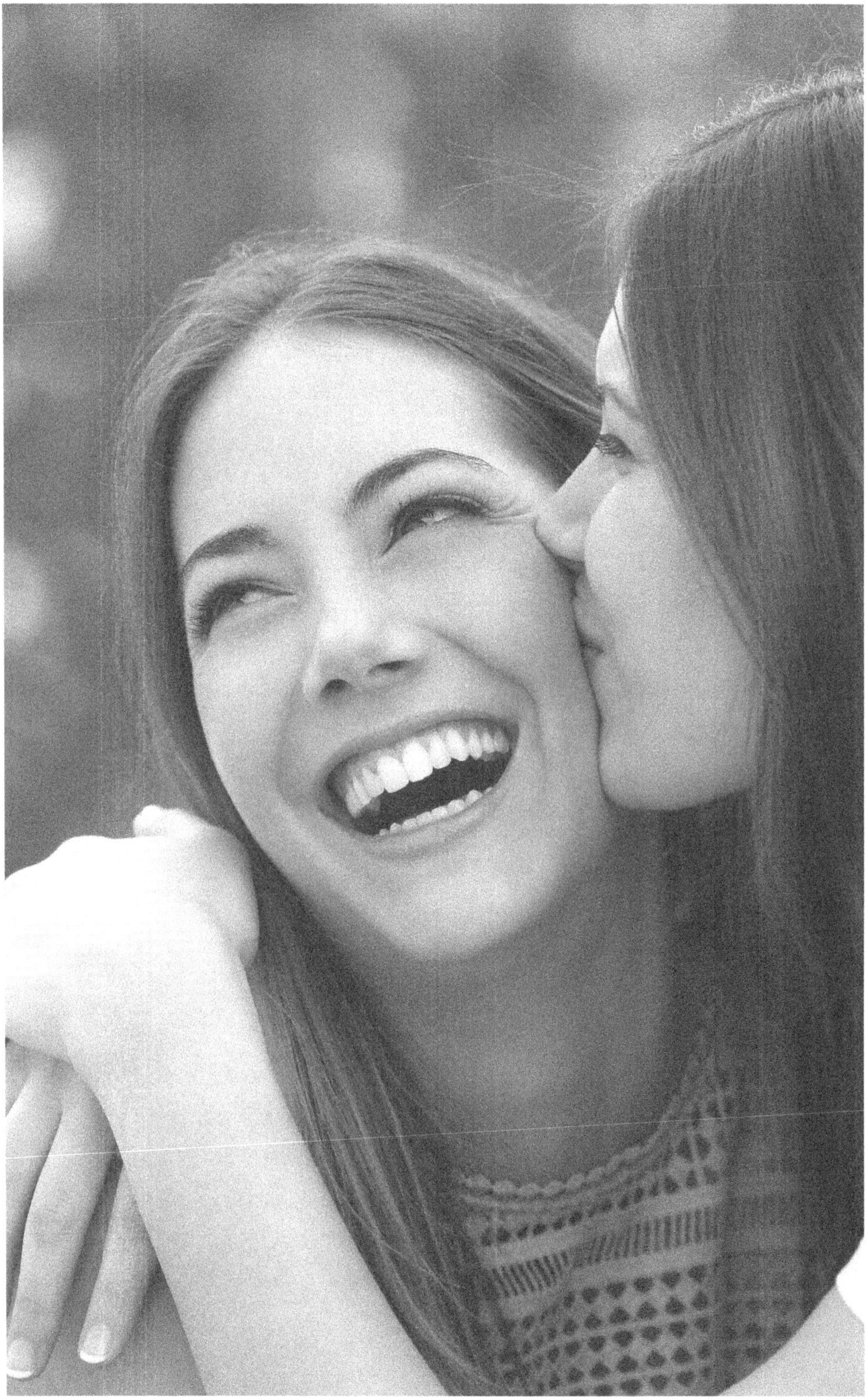

EIGHT
FIRST BASE

So now that you're all confident (don't even think about going to first base unless you know your self-worth), you're ready to notice and act upon your attractions.

We are attracted to a lot of people a lot of the time. We're almost always crushing on someone – a superstar, some kid in math class (hell, some kid in every class), our neighbour, our good 'friend'.

So how does this broad attraction change focus onto just one person? Who knows, but it does. For some it happens daily, for some it happens just a handful of times in their lives. One moment you are attracted to someone, the next you are attracted to a person who is attracted to you and both of you know it. Now the fun begins.

Somehow you and that person are face to face, or ear to phone, or eye to screen. Regardless, you and the other are going to exchange words. Maybe you're already friends. Maybe you've never met.

Anyway, attraction leads to engagement. (No, not as in a wedding!) One of you speaks to the other. The words are lame like, 'Hey, wassup?' 'Not much.' 'I see you in biology.' Blah, blah, blah.

What's really being said is between the bodies. 'Hey, I think you're hot.' 'I've been thinking about you for a long time.' 'You think I'm hot?' 'You noticed me before?' 'You won't hurt me, right?' 'God, I want to touch your hair, kiss your neck ...'

Right then, right at that silent thought, the other, the object of your attraction, throws back her beautiful hair and exposes her neck, even though in real talk she just said, 'You're on the volleyball team, right?'

Weird, huh? With attraction and engagement, words go out the window and unspoken communication becomes loud. Sometimes everyone in the room can hear it.

So depending on the circumstances, you'll either keep this going or move apart. For example, if you're at someone's house and curfew is hours away, you'll keep it going. If you just had a few minutes in study hall and the bell rings, the moment has passed, but the door is now open. Using the baseball metaphor: you just hit a single. You made it to first base. The door is open. You are attracted and you are engaging each other. No touch. Maybe a playful bump or wrestle, but there's no commitment of romance or sexuality. No kiss. No handhold. There is now the potential for something more.

First base is what most of the romance in books and movies is all about. There's an attraction. They part. Another encounter. They smile ... they know. They part. They are just about to kiss, something happens, something gets in the way. They part. They meet again. Someone lies to them about the other. They are confused. They part. They misunderstand. They stay away from each other. They find out the truth about the other. They almost kiss again. They part, and then finally – oh-my-god, wait for it, wait for it – they kiss. Ah. How many movie-watching hours have we spent waiting in first base? We just love it! It's the same formula over and over again. But we don't care – we love it!

FiRST BASE iS WHAT MOST OF THE ROMANCE iN BOOKS AND MOVIES iS ALL ABOUT.

Let's face it, most sexual encounters don't get past first base. Still, first base is a blast. And hopefully you make it to first base a zillion times in your life.

But at that moment – the purposeful touch, a kiss, a handhold, an arm around the waist, a hug with a kiss on the top of the head – then, and only then, do you advance to second base.

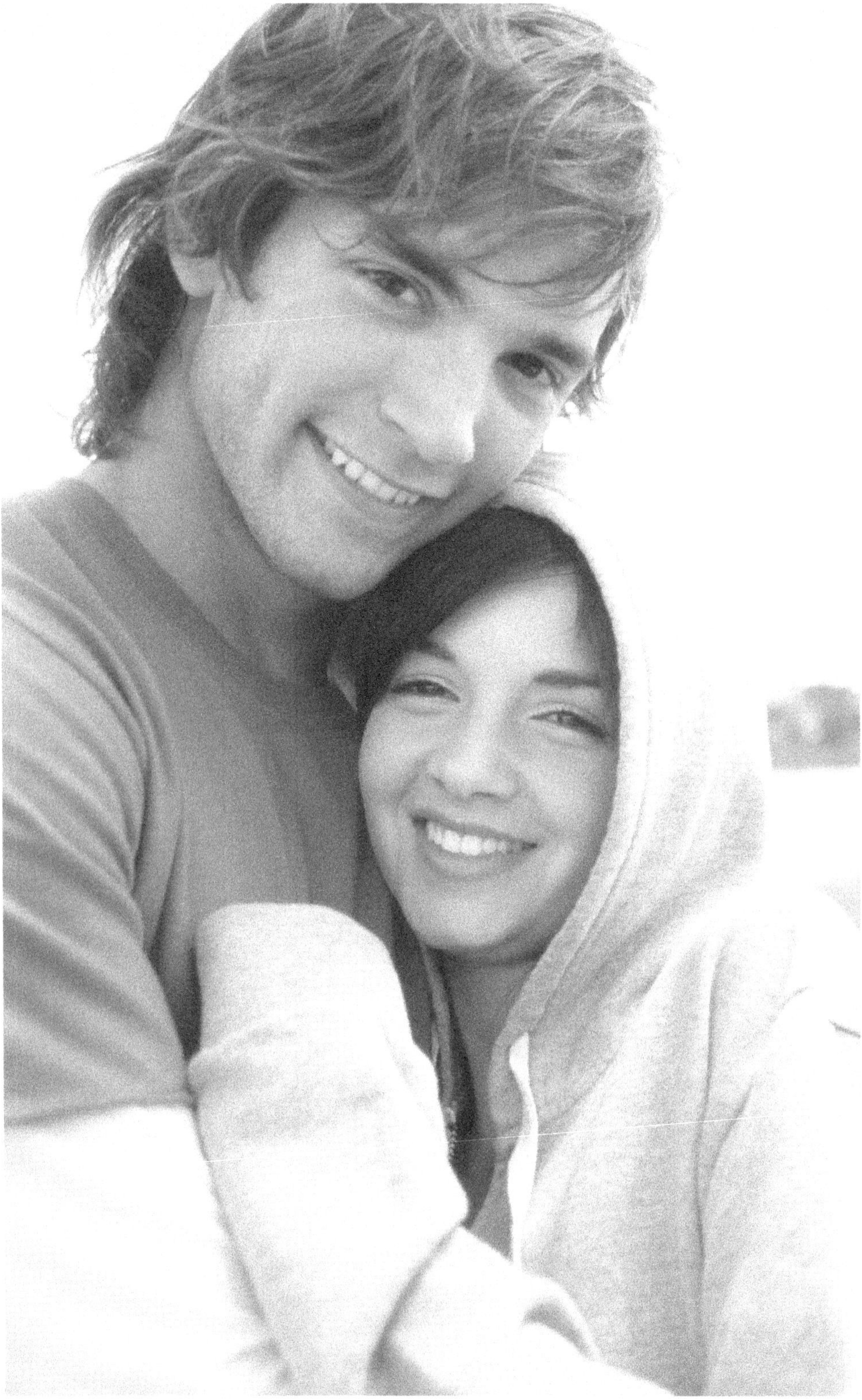

NINE
SECOND BASE

Second base is the one most often skipped by our generation. One girl put it so perfectly: 'You fool around. You don't really kiss until after you've done a lot of stuff or have sex. You kiss only if you really like someone.'

'But you can fool around with just anyone?' I asked.

'Oh, yeah. Kissing is more intimate.'

How messed up is that?

I like kissing.

I like kissing a lot.

There are a lot of great kissing scenes in movies. Look for them to remind you why great kisses are vital to great romantic and sexual relationships. Never, ever compromise on a kiss.

Second base is all about touch. Holding hands, embracing, kissing, French kissing, hands up and down the back, chests and pelvises pressed against each other, clothing always between flesh. Lots of non-verbal stuff going on.

Bodies wake up. Groins wake up.

Lots of dancing is a second-base kind of sexuality. Holding waists, grinding against each other (though the pure 'grinding' dancing is great for guys, it does absolutely nothing for girls!), kissing softly on the mouth, pelvis finding pelvis like magnets.

Second base is the base teens need to know about, honour, master and linger on.

SECOND BASE IS ALL ABOUT TOUCH.

At second base, you have a slightly better chance at *scoring* than you did at first. But more than likely, you'll spend the whole inning there. You should have a blast while you wait.

The art to second base is in the lingering. It is in the body building in excitement, then slowing down. It is in the nibbled ear, the kiss on the neck, the forehead touching forehead. The divine acknowledging the divine.

You could say, 'I'm staying at second base for a long time. Until I'm eighteen/in love/married.' In fact I know a girl who tells everyone that she only kisses. She proclaims it all the time, like she's wearing a bumper sticker that says, 'I kiss. I like to kiss. I only kiss.' She loves to kiss. And she has kissed her fair share of boys. But she sets the limit before spit gets swapped.

If a boy starts putting their hands on her body she stops kissing and says, 'Nope!' And that's it. She leaves. She is a famous kisser in her town. A friend of mine kissed her once at a party. He said it was so fun just kissing, knowing that was all that was going to happen. He loved kissing her because he knew the line.

Sadly, we were taught by porn that all excitement must quickly lead to sex. It doesn't. There are lots of things you can do when you get sexually excited. You can practise the art of calming down the energy created on second base. You can use that energy on all sorts of things from cleaning your room, running a few miles or practising some of those Sixty-Four Sacred Arts. And once you get back home, you can also release that energy through self-pleasure. There are many options.

SADLY, WE WERE TAUGHT BY PORN THAT ALL EXCITEMENT MUST QUICKLY LEAD TO SEX. IT DOESN'T.

But remember this! You need to linger on second base a long time in order to know how you feel about the person you are with. Besides being attracted, ask yourself if you like this person. Do you respect this person?

Does he/she try and go too fast, too slow? Does he/she have any mastery over their sexuality? Are they kind? What sorts of relationships have they had in the past? Can you talk about sexuality with them? Are they self-confident? Do they like you or do they simply want to 'get' you? Be honest about how attracted you are as you play on second base. How's the kissing? What's happening or not happening to your body?

I'd never go further than second base unless I'd gone there many, many times with someone. Go to second base again and again until you know you want to go further. The next bases are significantly more vulnerable. Your trust in yourself and in your partner needs to be very high. Your feelings about going further need to be very strong.

Second base is the base of romance. It is the part that happens after that first kiss. These moments are the ones we remember forever; not so much the more sexual moments. And that says something. Consider. A man told me about his first date with the woman who is now his wife.

> *We went to this animation festival. In the dark of the theater I took her hand and held it for about an hour. Then I began rubbing it with my thumb. I wanted her to know how much I liked her. We touched fingertips, interlocked fingers. Finally, I brought her hand to my lips. I turned it over so I could kiss the middle of her palm. She pulled our hands to her mouth. Then she put one of the tips of my fingers into her mouth. I will always remember that moment. I went crazy. That's all we did that night: hold and kiss hands. That's how I knew I'd marry her. We still spend a lot of time holding and kissing hands.*

Our sex lives will be revolutionised if we can learn to linger at second. This is the base of knowing the other. DO NOT SKIP IT! Don't simply tag the base and sprint to third. Build the excitement. Let your body get aroused. Back away from the arousal. Let it get aroused again and again.

At some point you'll decide you are ready to go further. You'll grab your partner's hand and you'll head for third base.

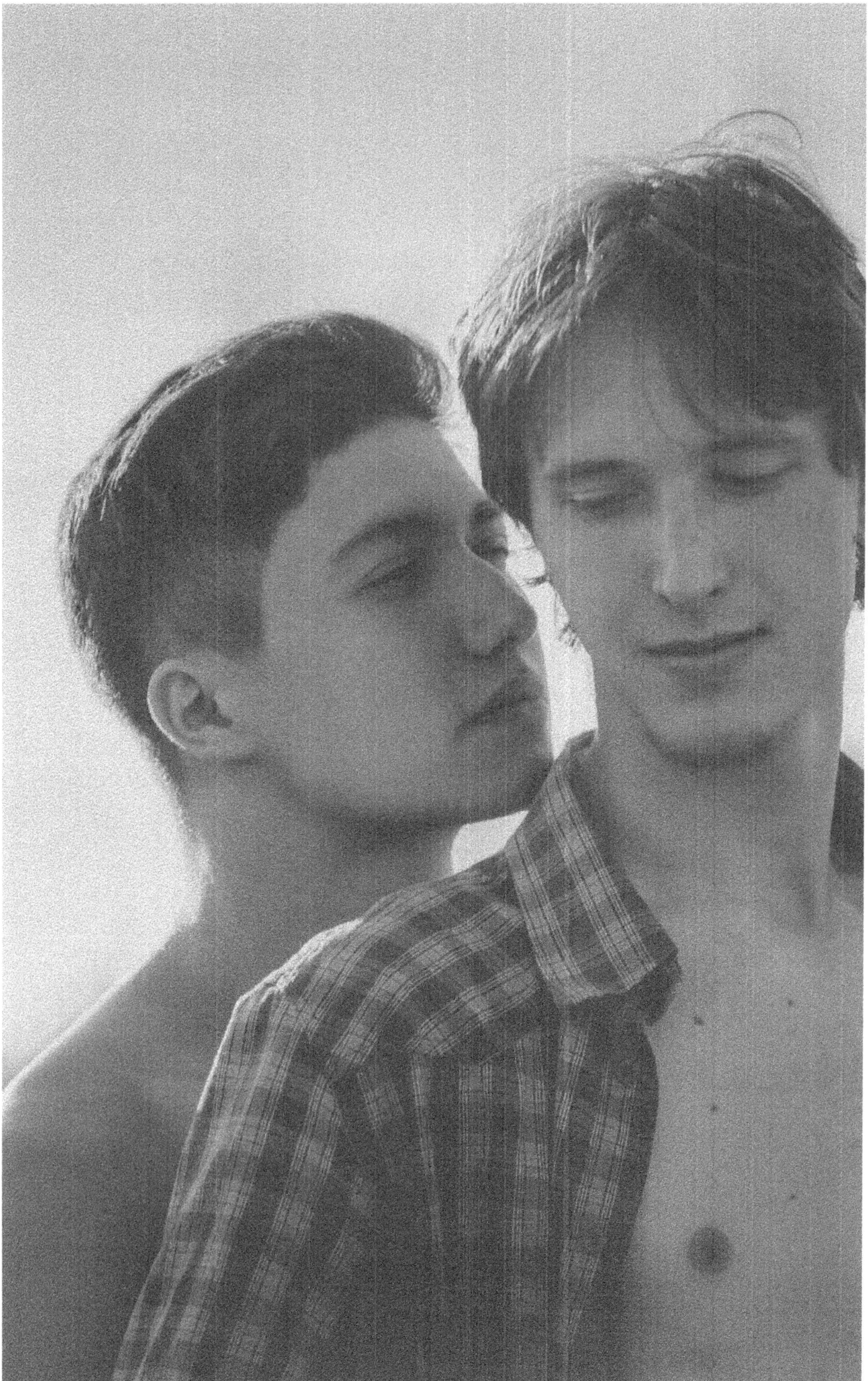

TEN
THIRD BASE

Ah, third base. In a mindful world, we'd linger at first and go to second only if we're completely comfortable with ourselves and the other. We'd enjoy second to the fullest. We'd allow our bodies to enjoy without forcing or rushing. We'd use second base to learn about ourselves, to grow up and get older, to deepen our connection and build our desire while we are being honest about the other, the circumstances, the timing and our safety.

If all is well, we'd jog over to third.

Unlike its baseball metaphor, third base requires fewer clothes than the first two bases. Inhibitions disappear. Hand, tongues, mouths explore the other to a tremendous building of excitement and want.

Everyone I interviewed reported they would like to play at third, even though it is assumed that if you do the things we do on third base you will be having sex. They said they would like to try stuff without assuming they had to go all the way. They'd like to go forward and backward.

They'd also like to orgasm without actual sex. They'd like to orgasm by grinding into each other, by hands or fingers, by oral sex. They'd like to do everything but have intercourse. For some reason, this is less acceptable than it was in the past. Almost everyone interviewed thought if you went to third base you were obligated to go Home. You aren't.

Until recently, teens fooled around a lot, but a lot of them didn't have actual sex. They did 'everything but … ' I interviewed many adults who said they tried so many sexual things for months, even years. Overall, they reported their first actual experience of sex was far better than the actual sex of teens today. Why? Because they went slowly through the bases and got to know their bodies.

I've heard adults complain that kids are having oral sex in order to avoid having actual intercourse. This is interesting because most sexually active adults have tried, if not continued, to have oral sex. I think the real issue is whether both partners want to try it.

Many teen girls I spoke to said they have given oral sex. Some enjoyed it. They felt safer about oral sex than actual sex. Some felt pressured and hated it. A lot of girls didn't want the boy to orgasm in their mouth. They didn't even know that they could have told the boys they didn't want that to happen. They needed to be able to tell their partner what they wanted ahead of time.

WE NEED TO BE ABLE TO TELL OUR PARTNERS WHAT WE WANT AHEAD OF TIME …

Mindful sex is a pattern of first base to a slow second to a very slow third. So if you're going to fool around, if you're gonna play ball, if you want to master sex, then practise. Have a partner you can practise with. Talk directly about going forward or easing off. Talk about how far is the furthest you want to go. Master your desires. Master your excitement.

Master your desires. Master your excitement.

It is important to note that just because your partner wants to go to Second or Third or Home Base doesn't mean you have to or maybe even want to.

Third Base really requires the skill of being able to say and hear 'No.' (See Chapter 12)

Third Base is tricky. Be safe. Be careful. Be sure of yourself. Be sure of your ability to stop when and where you want to stop. Be sure you trust your partner.

Be sure you trust your partner.

Be sure because a Home Run is just a sprint away.

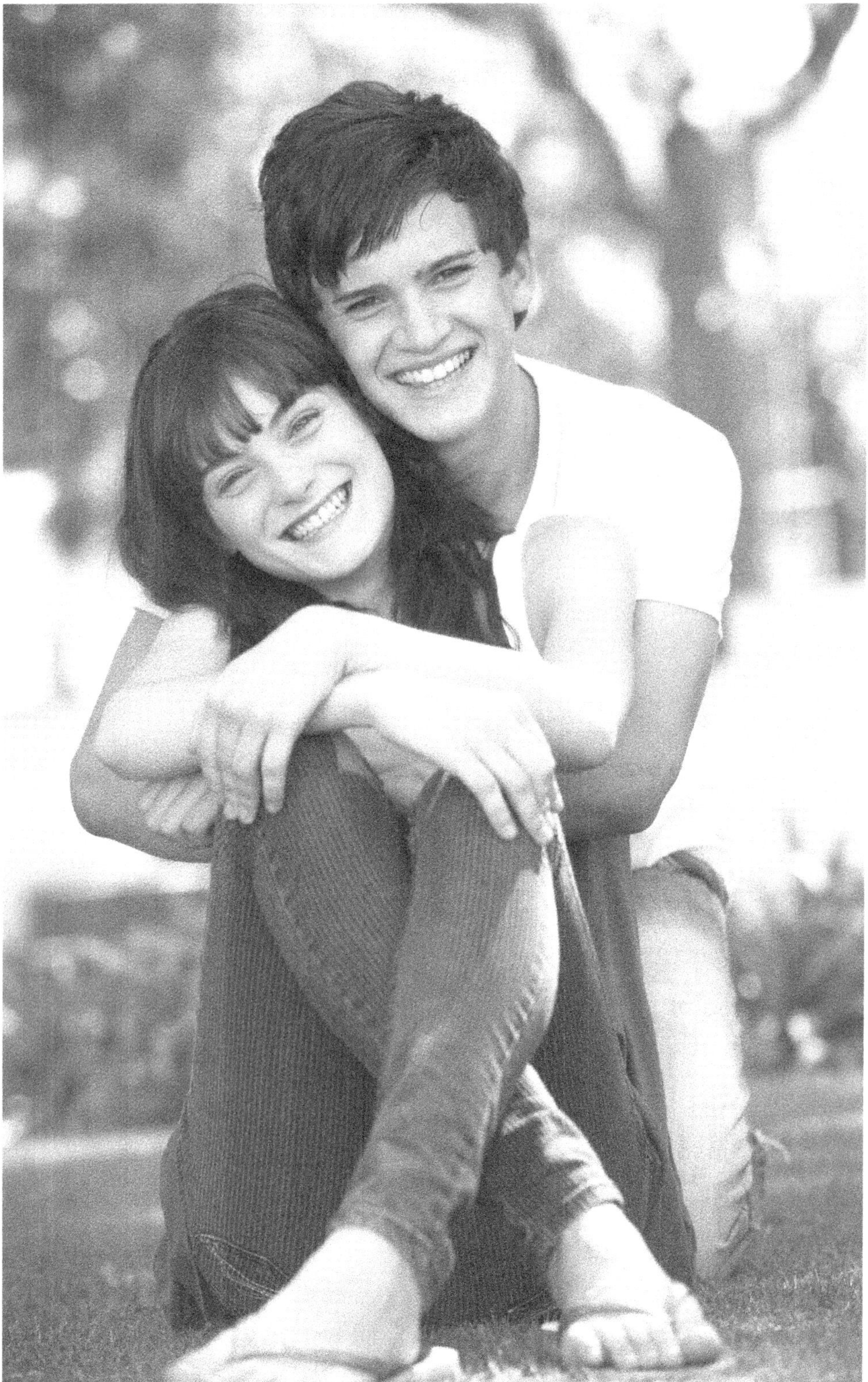

ELEVEN
THE HOME RUN

It's pretty simple. Traditionally: penis in vagina. (Gay mechanics are a bit modified, but it's the same idea of genitals on/in genitals.)

Find pictures from tantric texts or from *The Kama Sutra*. You can see them online or at any bookstore. The ancient drawings are explicit, yet the faces are calm, the eyes focused on the other. The pace is not frantic. It is beautiful.

Until sex can be like that, don't do it. Have fun. Self-pleasure, but don't have bad sex. Bad sex can taint your whole future sex life.

If you can't stare into the eyes of your partner, clean and clear, guilt-free, full of desire, respect, trust, joy, love, playfulness and creativity, then don't do it. Because someday you will be able to.

My favorite teen sex scene is from an old movie called *Say Anything*. Even though the sex occurs in the back seat of a car, the couple is certain of their actions. They are respectful and responsible. They stare deeply into each other's eyes. (Check 'sex scene from *Say Anything*' on YouTube.)

Here's a Home Run checklist.

* How long have you known each other?
* How sober are you?
* Are you able to talk about what might happen?
* How safe is the environment?
* How safe is your body?
* Can you look into the eyes of the other?
* How aroused is your body? Is it ready?
* What does your inner voice say?
* How will you feel after?

If you scored a Home Run, I hope it was good. I hope you really liked your partner. I hope you were so responsible you know your body is safe. I hope you had an orgasm. I hope you are still smiling big. I hope this is the beginning of a fabulous sex life to go with your fabulous life.

If not, no worries. Stop. Go back to the beginning and slowly become a master. It is not over. Heal up. Take your time. Use the experience to do it differently. Slowly.

Do not, really, do not keep having sex just because you've had sex once. Don't stay with the partner if it was bad, or if you don't really like that person anymore. Don't force the relationship. It seldom gets better. Sex is too intimate to compromise.

The sensitivity and delicacy of the skin in the vagina melded with the sensitivity of the penis makes sex so vulnerable. This is not like the other bases. It is not like holding hands. Bodies are interlocked.

Fluids are colliding on a cellular level, condom in-between or not. New electrical currents are being made. Sex is amazing. Honour it. Master it. Be very, very selective.

As Cher's wise character in the wonderful movie *Clueless* says, 'You know how picky I am about my shoes, and they only go on my feet.'

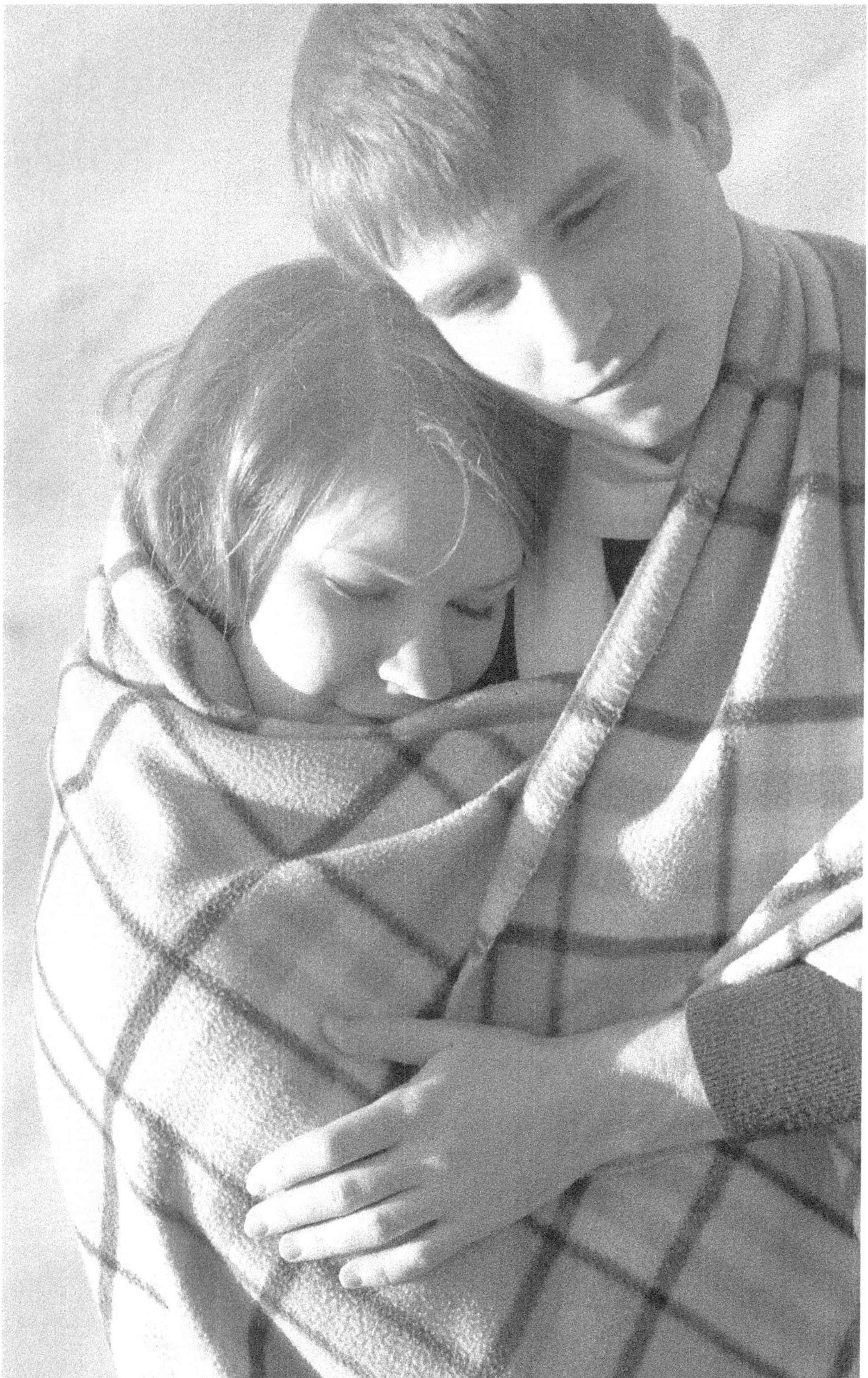

TWELVE
KNOW *THE NO*

I'm ending the section on The Bases with a discussion on the 'No'. The Bases are all about the yes *and the* no.

It isn't easy saying 'No' in the middle of a serious make-out session. It isn't always easy hearing your partner say 'No'. Sexuality is for when you are old enough, and mature enough, healed enough to know how to say 'No'. To say 'No' when you need to, and to know when your partner is saying '*No*'.

SEXUALITY IS FOR WHEN YOU ARE OLD ENOUGH, AND MATURE ENOUGH, HEALED ENOUGH TO KNOW HOW TO SAY '*NO*' .... AND TO KNOW WHEN YOUR PARTNER IS SAYING '*NO*'.

There are signs that your partner is saying 'No' without using words. One of the first signs that your partner is saying 'No' is that they are not moving forward with you. You are moving them forward. They are not pulling your body to theirs, they stop initiating kissing, they are not removing their clothing, and they are not smiling or laughing or talking or making 'mmm' sort of sounds. They have grown silent and cold. They are not initiating anything. They are have become like rag dolls.

They are clearly saying 'No'!

It is a great idea to do some groundwork before you go out with someone. Talk about what you would want to do or not do *before* the date. It helps a lot if you have had some conversation before you are alone and start playing ball, because if your partner starts trying to do things you don't want to do, you can say, 'Hey, we talked about this.'

I love talking with kids who are very, very comfortable with drawing their lines. They say things like, 'Are you kidding me?' and 'I told you what I was willing to do!' and 'Pretty sure we both agreed on this … ' Some, like Joe, are pretty sweet about, 'This isn't gonna happen.'

Practise how to say 'I'm not comfortable with that.' 'I don't know you that well.' 'I want to know you better.' Or simply, 'No'.

> **PRACTISE HOW TO SAY 'I'M NOT COMFORTABLE WITH THAT.' 'I DON'T KNOW YOU THAT WELL.' 'I WANT TO KNOW YOU BETTER.' OR SIMPLY, 'NO.'**

KNOW THE NO

If you are with a partner worthy of any romantic and sexual encounter, they will join you in some talk.

- 'Is this okay?'
- 'What would you like to try?'
- 'Can I try this?'
- Not the basic: 'Oh baby, you're so sexy.' Or 'I love you' (when you just met). Or, 'I want you so bad.'

If your partner is not answering your questions, that is a 'No'. If your partner shrugs or says, 'I don't know,' that is a 'No'. If your partner says, 'I don't care,' that is a 'No'. Even if your partner says an unenthusiastic, 'Sure,' that is a 'No'. An unenthusiastic anything is a 'No'.

AN UNENTHUSIASTIC ANYTHING IS A 'NO'.

The most obvious and least talked about non-verbal *'No. I'm not ready for this'* sign for boys is that their penises are not hard, and for girls their vaginas are not lubricated. These are absolute, clear signs that your partner is not ready to be doing whatever you are doing. Stop. Pull back. Put your clothes back on. Figure out why you or they aren't ready. Maybe you are too young. Maybe you don't really like or trust the person you are with. Maybe you are feeling too guilty. Maybe you just haven't been playing ball long enough.

NOTE: Just because a penis is hard or a vagina is wet doesn't mean the partner is saying, 'Yes!'

Even when the body might be saying Yes, I'm aroused, we still may not want to go further. And all the rules or 'No' still apply.

I heard terrible stories from some girls who were in the first few minutes of kissing and the boy put his hands down their pants and stuck his fingers into their very dry vaginas. Here they are, barely on Second Base and he's acting like they are on Third heading into Home. It was absolutely no fun at all. The girls felt violated. It hurt. Some stopped the encounter. Some kept going because they thought if they had gone that far they were obligated to go all the way. They weren't!

A lot of girls believe that sexy girls are ready for anything, anytime. (I blame this on porn!) They believe sexy girls never say 'No'. They are so misinformed. Truly sexy girls love their bodies and their sexuality, and they will say 'No' anytime things are not right.

Saying 'No' when you don't want to do something sexual is a sign that you adore yourself and you know your worth. Not trying to make someone do what they don't want to do is a sign that you know the worth of another.

NOT TRYING TO MAKE SOMEONE DO WHAT THEY DON'T WANT TO DO IS A SIGN THAT YOU KNOW THE WORTH OF ANOTHER.

Knowing when you want to say 'No', saying it and listening when others say it is one of the best antidotes for the poison of porn. It is one of the best skills to happiness, because when you can say 'No' during an intimate sexual moment, you can probably say 'No' anytime.

WHEN YOU CAN SAY 'NO' DURING AN INTIMATE SEXUAL MOMENT, YOU CAN PROBABLY SAY 'NO' ANYTIME.

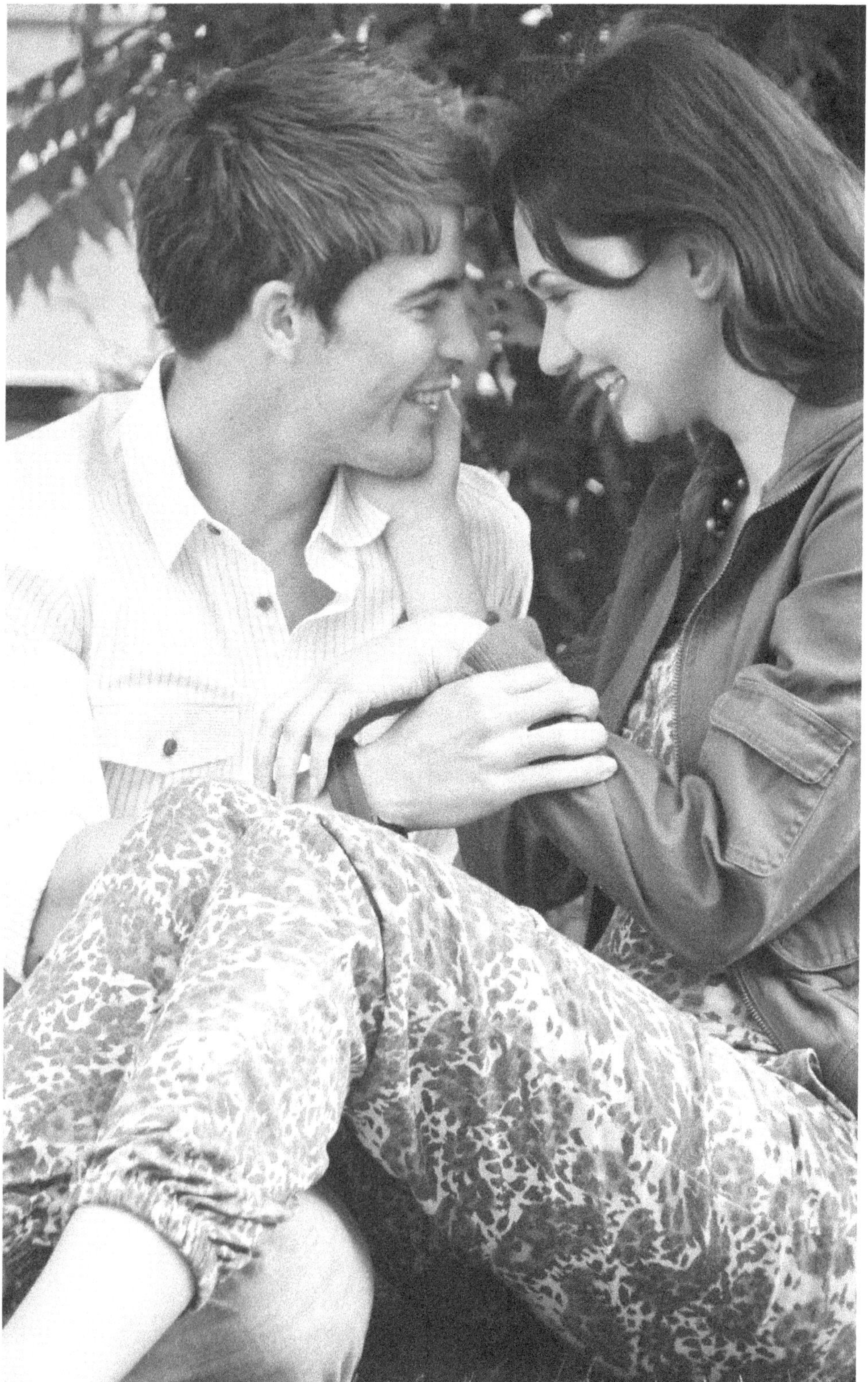

PART THREE
KNOW THE REST

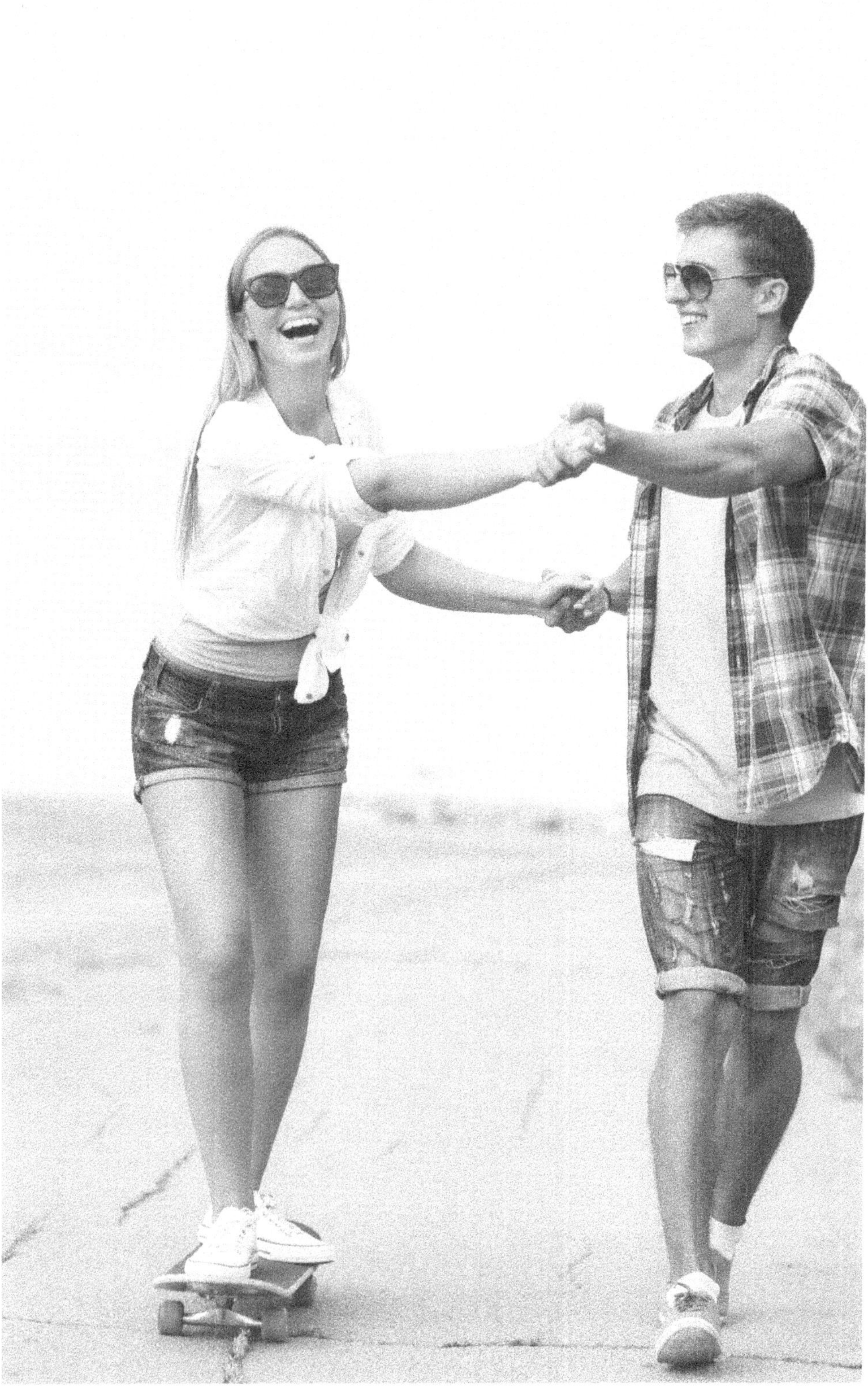

THIRTEEN
FLIRTING

Flirting is one of the best things in life. You can't talk about the rest without talking about the best first.

I love to flirt.

Flirting is not just for romance and sex. Flirting is for everyone. Babies flirt with us in restaurants. Dogs flirt with us when they wag their tails. Hummingbirds flirt with the very air. I flirt every time I notice some beautiful, fun and connecting energy and I decide to play with it.

What is flirting? How can we spot it? How can we get really good at it? Why would we want to?

Two images come to mind when I think of flirting. First, I envision flirting as playing together with energy, like kicking a hacky-sac, like soaring a frisbee across a freshly cut lawn, like shooting water guns on a hot summer night. There is a lot of laughter, smiling and rising to the occasion. We double dare each other to be creative, cute and clever. We ask the other to bring out the best in us.

It doesn't matter if it is in-person or through an adorable text or within cyber *poke, like, friending,* or *wink*, because when we flirt we are really saying, *I like you, I am thinking about you, you're awesome, let's play.*

The second image I have of flirting is surfing. You catch the massively fun energy of a wave and ride it. You see it coming and you start paddling to join the energy of the wave. You don't try and control it, you just ride it. If you love surfing, there are and always will be waves to catch, because every minute of every day there are millions of waves building behind millions of waves that are high-fiving the shore. There are always flirting waves of energy to catch because the desire to connect playfully is always deep within all of us.

THERE ARE ALWAYS FLIRTING WAVES OF ENERGY TO CATCH BECAUSE THE DESIRE TO CONNECT PLAYFULLY IS ALWAYS DEEP WITHIN ALL OF US.

As fun as flirting is, it gets bad press. Flirters are frequently judged by others. I think it's because flirting sparks jealousy. When we flirt the energy that is usually spread out to everyone focuses like a laser beam on one or a few people. If that laser beam isn't on us, we feel left out.

Sometimes the people who feel left out will judge the flirters. They say things like, 'She's such a flirt!' or 'He's such a player.' Flirters are often gossiped about by those who feel left out. This happens so often that flirting is considered a negative thing. It is as if all flirters are just moments away from being sexually inappropriate.

They aren't. Flirting is great. Flirting is just playing with our energy. Just playing.

So try not to judge those who are flirting. Just notice that you feel left out when others are flirting. Try to remember how great it feels when you are flirting. Don't hurt the flirters with gossip. Be happy for them. Join them if you can. On the flip side, when you are flirting, try to include more people. Notice if anyone is feeling left out. It's easy to include others. Get good at flirting.

First remember that we are all born knowing how to flirt. The easiest way to catch that flirt wave is to remember the perfect and equal worth of the other. When we do this, the other usually looks for the best in us. The easiest was for people to see the best in us is for us to mirror their worth back to them. Super simple.

> **THE EASIEST WAY TO CATCH THAT FLIRT WAVE IS TO REMEMBER THE PERFECT AND EQUAL WORTH OF THE OTHER.**

Flirting. Do it. Do it often. Notice when someone is inviting a flirt. Their eyes meet yours and they smile. They text something funny. They bump you playfully with their shoulder. They notice you. They tease you. Watch how you respond to them. Trust your gut. If you don't feel right about the person, if they are making you feel uncomfortable, like they want something from you, or you are not enjoying the flirt, then don't flirt back. But, if you trust them and you want to play a little, tease them, relax and enjoy.

Flirting is fleeting. Like butterflies and rainbows, it only lasts a little while. Don't grip it. Don't start thinking about being BFFs or marriage as you toss the energy back and forth. When the moment begins to lose its momentum, be grateful. Then get your board and head back into the ocean to catch the next wave.

Lots of flirting is not sexual or romantic, yet the best romances start with great flirting. If there is flirting and a hint of sexuality or romance (or the best, romantic sexuality) then, my friend, you are on First Base.

Great romance needs a lot of energy. Flirting provides it. Whenever I flirt I leave the moment feeling all filled up. I'm happy. I am content. I know my worth deeply. In what better soil can a romance grow?

Flirting is all about loving the life in others. It is about being present right here, right now. We can flirt away a whole lot of problems like hatred, loneliness and self-doubt. We can flirt our way into some great romances and smiling kisses. Like the hokey-pokey: *that's what it's all about*!

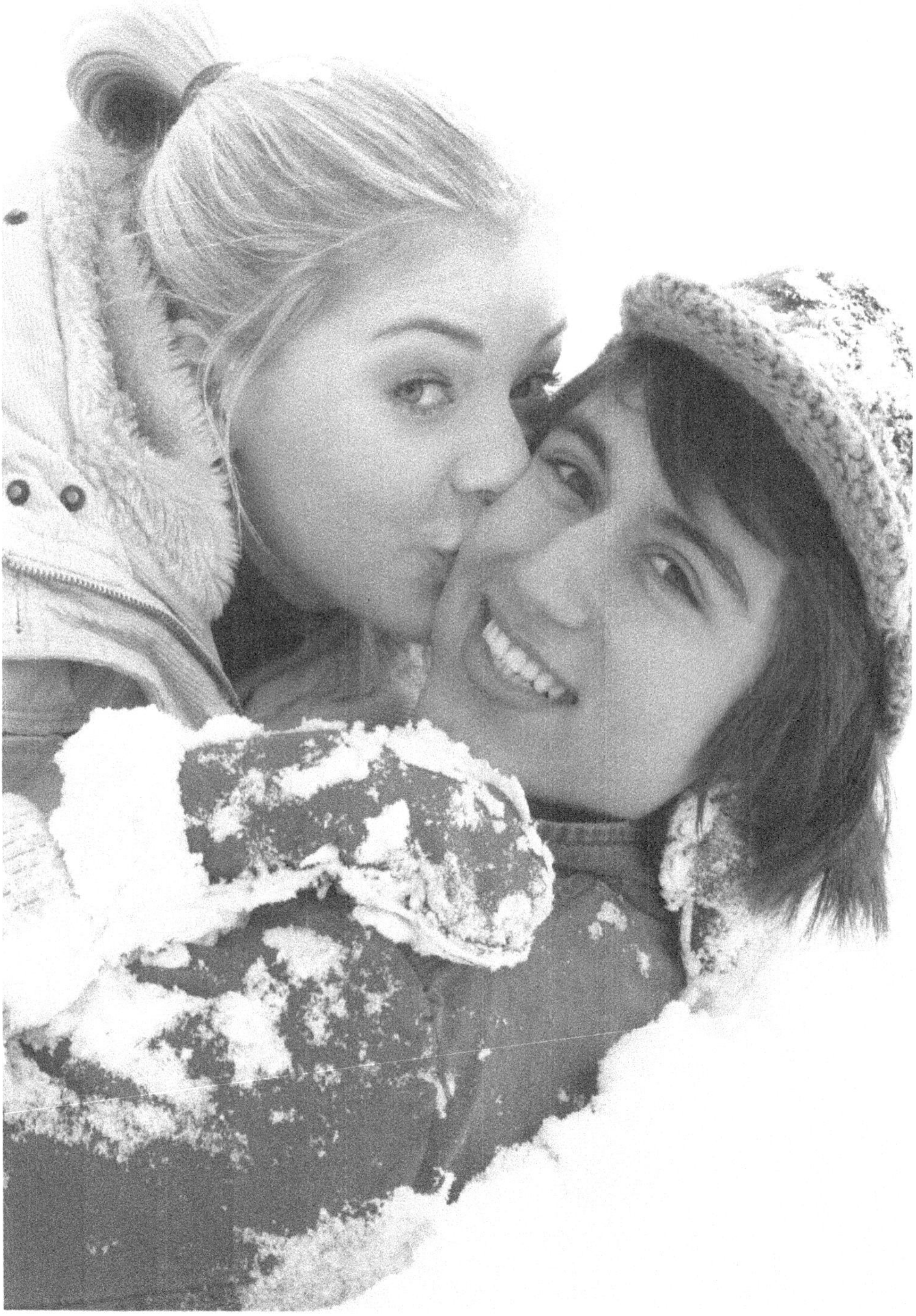

FOURTEEN
VIRGINITY IS NOT A BACKPACK

What an odd thing virginity is. One minute you're a virgin, the next you aren't. One simple action. Does that go for the other orifices? Are you a virgin nose picker until you first put your finger up your nose? Do you have virgin ears until you use a cotton-bud?

Having sex is an amazingly personal thing – but our generation talks about it like we talk about our backpacks. You have it. You lose it. Your friends want you to lose it or keep it. It's a burden. It defines you.

In reality, sex is an experience, not a possession. Almost everyone I've talked with said the actual moment of losing it was such a let-down compared to what everyone thought it would be. When I was younger, I thought the moment I lost my virginity my life would change from Dorothy's black-and-white Kansas to the brilliant colour of the Land of Oz.

To be honest, that is what happened when I had my first orgasm with Joe, and that wasn't sex. I was still a virgin, yet for a long while the colours were brighter; the world more magical.

In the book *Memoirs of a Geisha*, there is a huge commotion over which man will be able to pay the highest bid to have sex with the virgin geisha. This goes on for months. The entire time the girl is terrified, but preparing herself. Finally this one guy pays a ton of money. The girl waits alone in a room, lying down on a mat. The guy comes in, gets on top of her, penetrates her, moves around a little, and then comes in an instant.

The best part of the whole thing is after he leaves, she is sitting there with the masterful geisha and the two begin laughing at how ridiculous the whole things was – how much drama, money and preparation for such a shallow, unsatisfying and silly event.

The first time you have sex probably won't be the best thing that will happen in your life, but hopefully it won't be the worst. Certainly you can do lots to make sure it is a good experience. You can choose your partner wisely. You can make sure you are safe. You can make sure are really ready. You can study sexuality. You can know your body. You can take it real slow. You can make sure you have already mastered self-pleasure. You can get skilled in talking to your partner about sex. You can make sure you aren't harming your belief system.

THE FIRST TIME YOU HAVE SEX PROBABLY WON'T BE THE BEST THING THAT WILL HAPPEN IN YOUR LIFE.

Try not to make your first sexual experience one that will produce guilt, shame, embarrassment, fear, anger, disappointment, trauma or drama. These have nothing to do with sexuality as an art form. Why have sex if these will be the result?

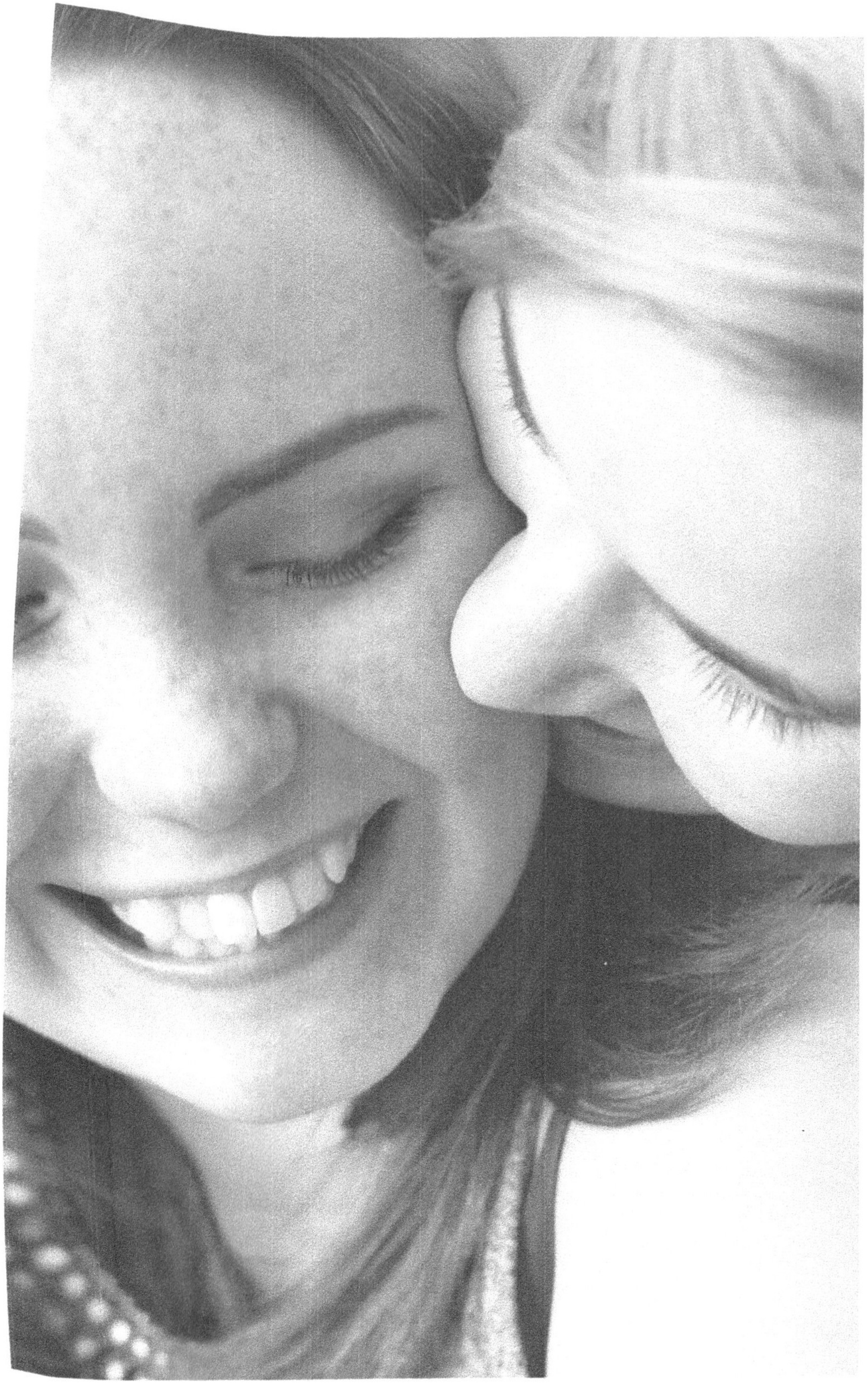

FIFTEEN
EXERCISE IN SELF-PLEASURE

I can't believe I am writing this, but really, someone has to talk about it! This is the part where we get specific about not letting anyone else teach you about your body but yourself. Besides, too many girls are not having orgasms. Too many boys self-pleasure mindlessly. This is a recipe for sexual disaster. So here goes.

First, for God's sake, make sure you are in some private place! Now, notice the emphasis on focus, on the building of excitement, on the slowing down and not just racing to the orgasm. Notice your entire body.

Think about something sexy: someone who turns you on, some great chest or abs, someone's flirty eyes or smile, some scene from a movie (not porn!) that stirs your body. Think of it.

Now, no matter what's going on down there and without touching yourself, focus on your circuitry. Feel the firing of electrical impulses from your groin to the rest of your body. Feel this. Notice your mind wanting to go further into the imagined sexual act. Note your hands are aching to touch yourself.

Don't.

Not yet.

Relax.

Notice.

Quiet your mind for a few minutes.

Now, think that sexy thought again. Touch yourself.

If you have self-pleasured before, you already know what feels good.

If you haven't, take your time.

There is a lot to explore.

Find the spots that thrill you, that heighten the tingling everywhere.

Then stop.

Move your hands to the rest of your body. Lightly touch every inch of yourself. Note the circuitry firing like tiny electric shocks. Find the areas that feel great.

Remember, take your time. Start and stop. Relax. Begin again. Notice your whole body. Notice your thoughts. What images or fantasies are flashing at you?

Go slow.

Build. Build. Build.

Discover your sexual body.

Make it come alive.

Find its pleasure.

At some point, you will pick up the pace. Your body will tense up. Even though your focus will be on your groin, notice the rest of your body and mind.

Do what feels great.

Build and build.

Before you release, be ready to notice the big bang throughout your entire body. Notice the pure peace and ecstasy and connectedness.

When you are there, release.

Oh … my … God!

Yep.

Feel your heart rate. Feel the blood coursing through your body. Feel the electricity flowing fast and pure and unblocked throughout your system. Feel the enormous pleasure of the release.

Know truths you often forget. Know you are not separate from anyone or anything. Know your infinite worth.

Practise. This is where your sexual energy needs to go first.

Know yourself.

Don't let some other teen try and teach you about yourself.

We might decide to wait to have sex, but we can certainly enjoy the pleasure of our bodies while we wait and learn and master this sacred art.

If you have a hard time having an orgasm with this exercise, there are some more specific ideas and exercises in *Our Bodies, Ourselves* by the Boston Women's Health Collective.

Or consider Daria Snadowski's great book *Anatomy of a Boyfriend* which is about a sweet couple discovering their sexuality, and issues about female orgasms. It's worth a look.

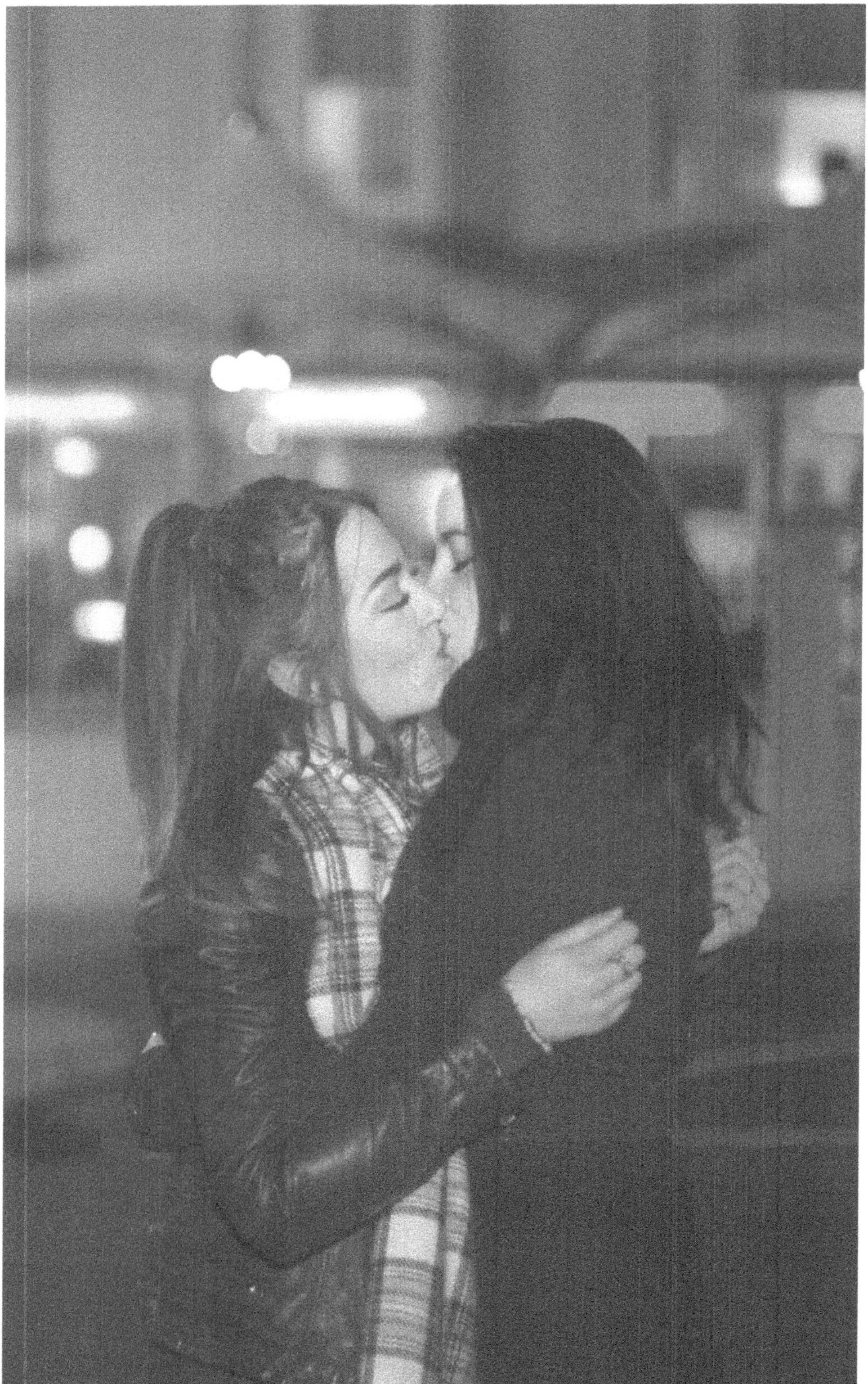

SIXTEEN
CYBER-SEXUAL CONNECTION

Let's face it, the cyber world is going to be part of our sexual world. I don't care what anyone says. It's available any time of day. The entire world is open to us. We can try all sorts of stuff we probably wouldn't in real life. Someone is always out there who thinks we are gorgeous, sexy, interesting. We can flirt with words or pictures or videos.

So, how do we do it well?

First – and this is vital – no matter how private it feels, *our cyber life is not private*. Not.

NO MATTER HOW PRIVATE IT FEELS, OUR CYBER LIFE IS NOT PRIVATE.

Remember, everything you post online is public. It doesn't matter whether or not you delete a message or text. If you've published it, it's traceable. When you post things online, you're creating a cyber fingerprint. And it seems that every year we find out more and more people are able to access our cyber information and history.

At some point we might not get into the college we wanted or get the job we interviewed for because some decision maker did a thorough search on us and found some horny moment from our past. Or worse, we don't try for things because we are afraid that someone might find out about something we did online. Or that we feel so embarrassed and exposed, we lose hope for love, romance and sexuality.

So, as with anything online, know that whatever you are doing may someday be seen by parents, partners, bosses, enemies, your children … even your grandchildren. Anything you wouldn't do in the middle of the halls at school probably shouldn't be done online either.

AS WITH ANYTHING ONLINE, KNOW THAT WHATEVER YOU ARE DOING MAY SOMEDAY BE SEEN BY PARENTS, PARTNERS, BOSSES, ENEMIES, YOUR CHILDREN … EVEN YOUR GRANDCHILDREN.

That being said, there are many amazing opportunities to connect with others online. But know that people can be different online to what they can be in real life. And discussions can get really intense. People can write such awesome stuff. They can say really nice things, things people don't usually say in person. They can seem so sexy. They can make you feel so sexy. And they can turn on a dime, and get mean and nasty.

I think both of these extremes can happen because there really are no consequences. So what, some random person that has no real pulse to them is in love, turned-on, hurt or angry? So what?

So just be real about the cyber world. It is real ... ish. There is a real person pushing the keys, telling you how great you are, talking about amazing things, making you and your body feel incredible. But it's sort of like putting a note into a bottle and tossing it into the ocean hoping it will find your soulmate. Probably not gonna happen. It's not likely that anything in the cyber world will become a person-to-person relationship. The cyber romantic and sexual world is sort of its own thing even though we keep pretending it is like life in the flesh.

Remember, you can't know if you really like someone you've only met online. It is body to body, eye to eye that tells you. Some great flirt online might do nothing for you in person. One of my friends met up with this guy she connected to online and was so disappointed by the flesh-and-blood guy who showed up. Even though he looked like his picture, he just didn't excite her at all. Attraction is all about flesh and blood.

REMEMBER, YOU CAN'T KNOW IF YOU REALLY LIKE SOMEONE YOU'VE ONLY MET ONLINE.

So let's make some ground rules. No nudes. No self-pleasure photos or videos. No real information like address, telephone number, school, even city. If you think you really like them then do a quick check on whether the information they give is real or not.

Be nice. There is a real person on the other end of that screen. There is so much cyber unkindness. Don't add to it. Don't participate in it.

Don't respond right away if you are really mad. Wait until you have cooled off. Too many cyber-wars have been started over a quick reaction to a salty text. We all know what a waste of energy this becomes.

Get rid of people who get way more sexual than you want. The easiest way is to simply block them. Blocking is one of the greatest things in the world. We can't just block real-life people. We have to deal with them, but anyone who annoys you online can be deleted from your world. There will be a lot of people you meet online who think you are there just to turn them on. It is sort of expected. So just block them the moment they ask. There will still be a million other people contacting you, just get rid of the bozos.

Another great trick, especially if the person who gets sexual online is someone you know, is to bring your parents into the equation. You can tell them that your parents read all your texts and that they better stop immediately. (Even if your parents don't, they could.) Or, one of my favorites. Ask your mum or dad if you can take a photo of them looking furious at you and send that to the cyber creep. Or, send the request from the cyber fool to all your friends. Chances are they are asking for the same things from them. It is a good social consequence.

Should you decide to meet the person in real life, treat it like you would any real date in real life. Let's be honest, if the person is good enough to meet in person you should be able to tell your parents about them and make sure they know you are going to meet them, just like other dates. Meet in public. Have a person you trust nearby in case you want to bail. Don't meet someone alone – EVER. If you meet them, and trust them, then treat the relationship like you would any other person you *just* met in real life. I don't care what you might have said or done online, they are a stranger until you get to know them.

I DON'T CARE WHAT YOU MIGHT HAVE SAID OR DONE ONLINE, THEY ARE A STRANGER UNTIL YOU GET TO KNOW THEM.

If you meet and don't like them, wave goodbye and block them forever. If they happen to be way older than they said they were, report them to the site immediately. If they are older and you were honest about your age and they got sexual with you online, report that to the police.

Another problem with getting really sexual online (besides the fact that *it isn't private*), is that you can get sort of addicted to sexual arousal. You can spend all your time and energy being sexually aroused by cyber folks. It gets in the way of homework and chores, but more importantly, it gets in the way of real-life relationships. They are harder, but way more important.

I say use the internet to flirt with people, to be more philosophical than you are in person, to argue your opinions, to bond over things you are geeky about like shows, books, superheroes. Attention is a blast. It is fun to be have someone out there to talk with every minute of every day. Just be mindful.

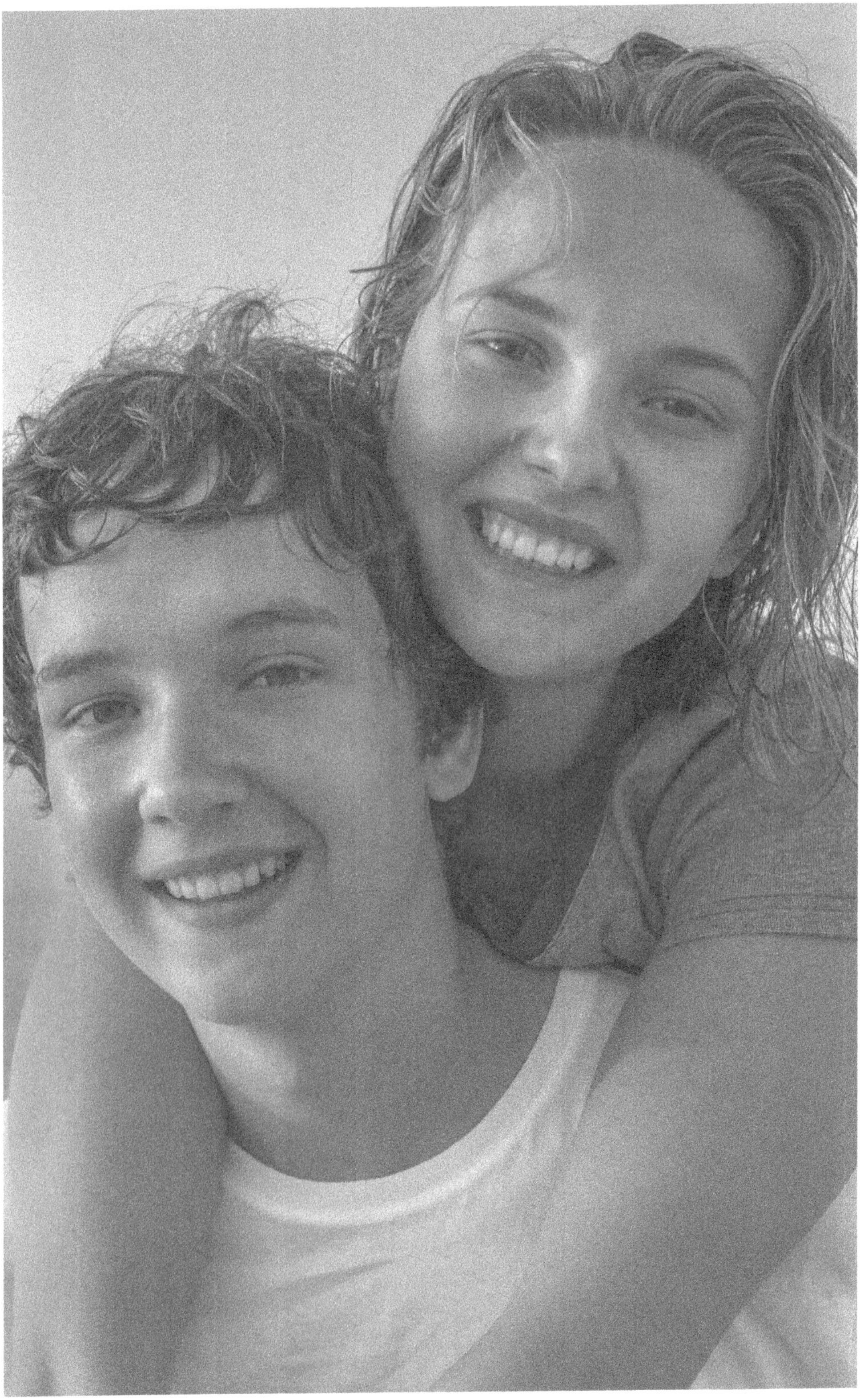

SEVENTEEN
CONNECT AND DISCONNECT

There is a belief in Zen buddhism that most people we encounter during our lives will come and go rather quickly. There will be a very few that last forever – family members, some best friends, husbands, wives, and children – but most people will come and go. This is natural. If we kept everyone forever, we'd be overwhelmed with the time and energy all those relationships would take.

Most relationships are moments. Good or bad; they end.

For some reason, when we really enjoy a moment with another person we have this need to make it last forever. We go from enjoying and seeing the best in the other to gripping, to expecting more than the moment.

Then, when the relationship ends, we decide we must feel terrible about it. We weep. We get angry. We decide that the person was never the great person we thought they were. We decide they lied or manipulated. We discount the moment we had. We doubt ourselves. And this happens tenfold, more, if attraction, romance, sexuality and especially sex, occurred during the relationship.

Let's face it, all sexual relationships do not end in marriage. In fact, only one or two will. Don't cling to relationships. Assume they will end sometime. Enjoy them. Don't pretend this cute boy won't move on in ten minutes or three weeks or six months. When you know this, you'll make informed sexual decisions.

There are guys and girls who act like they're going to marry every random person who flirts with them. I hear them crying when they've had sex with a well-known player who says 'I love you' before the first kiss, then disappears after the sexuality or sex. Their bad. Really, if you think someone is a player and is likely to move on quickly, decide if they're someone you want to be sexual with. Simple as that.

Be honest. Because most relationships are short, don't do things you only want to do with a really long-term relationship unless you've been together a really long time. Don't get all hurt when the flavour of the week moves on.

I hate it when people get mad and vengeful when things end, which we all know they will. They act like the nice moments were all fake and the guy or girl was really horrible when, in reality, most of those moments were real and nice and sacred. Just because they didn't end in a long-term relationship, the experience is made pathological. What a waste when we could have these awesome mental scrapbooks of sweet moments, but rip them to shreds instead. How messed up is that?

I say, take the high road. I love the saying, *The best revenge is good living.*

I HATE IT WHEN PEOPLE GET MAD AND VENGEFUL WHEN THINGS END, WHICH WE ALL KNOW THEY WILL ... I SAY, TAKE THE HIGH ROAD.

I have a friend who makes the boys she goes out with promise they will have *a mutual break-up*. They promise they won't lie to each other about their feelings. She thinks we all know when a break-up is inevitable. There is a magical shift and nothing – no kindness, no sex, no meanness, no threats, nothing – is going to repair it. So she and the guy promise when that happens they admit it and break up at the same time. So far it's worked perfectly.

Why don't we just admit when it's over? Do we really want to stay with someone forever even if it is clearly done, when the connection is broken?

Let's be the generation that quits being dramatically hurt when relationships end. Let's quit being vengeful. Let's quit cursing those souls we loved for a blessed moment.

LET'S BE THE GENERATION THAT QUITS BEING DRAMATICALLY HURT WHEN RELATIONSHIPS END. LET'S QUIT BEING VENGEFUL. LET'S QUIT CURSING THOSE SOULS WE LOVED FOR A BLESSED MOMENT.

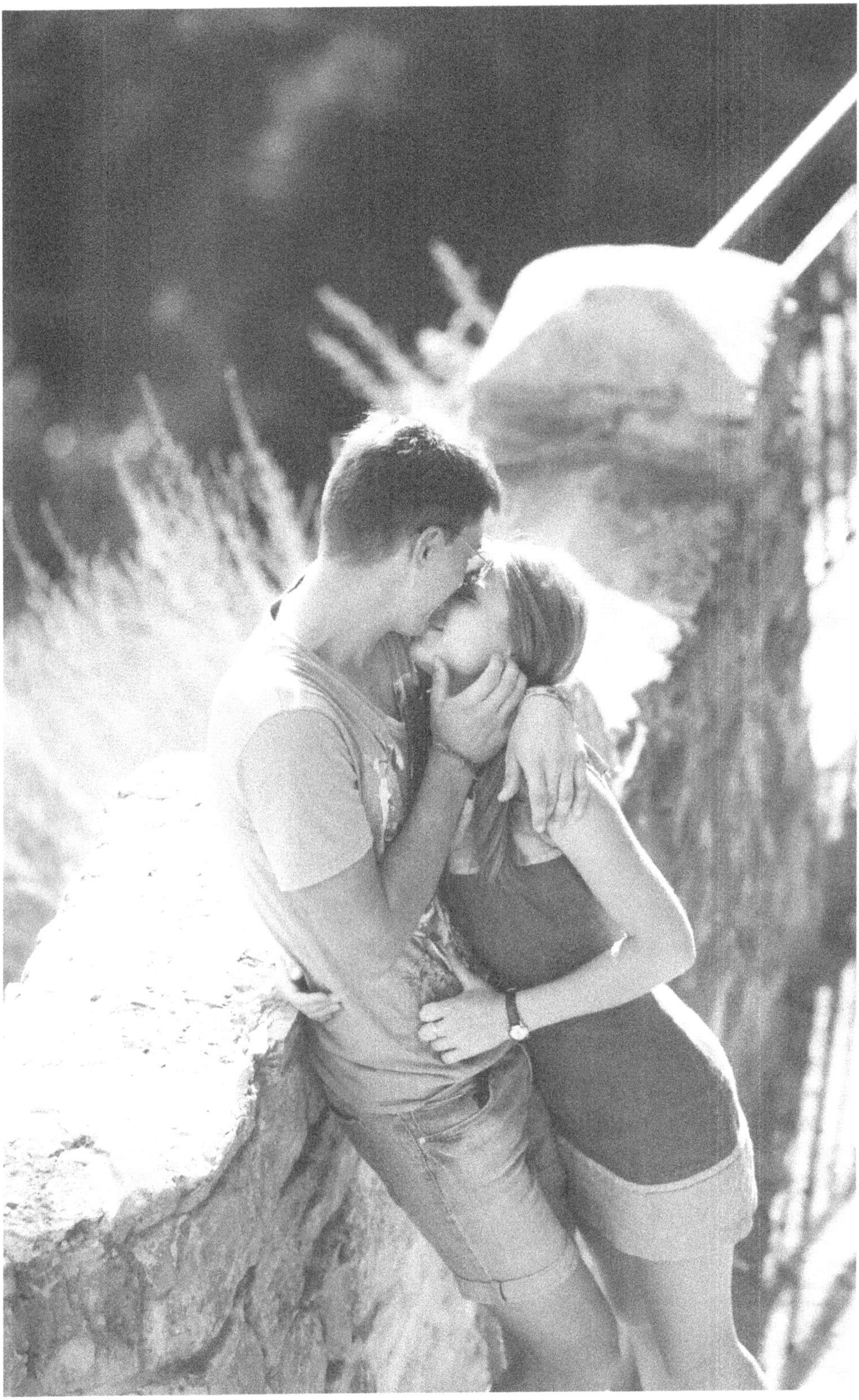

EIGHTEEN
SAFE SEX

Sexuality is a tricky thing. Though I hate all sex education that begins, ends and discusses only the safety aspects of sex, a sexual master must know the risks and take precautions.

Sex is risky because our bodies and feelings are so vulnerable. With any risky experience, you have to be prepared. You don't skydive without instruction and certainly not without a parachute. Likewise, you don't have sex without being safe, without protection, without responsibility.

The obvious risks of sex are going further than you want to go, sexual assault (see Chapter 19), pregnancy and sexually transmitted diseases (STDs). All of these can change your life forever. The younger you are when you become sexually active, the higher your risk of these occurring. This is important.

This chapter is not a manual on safe sex because one chapter just can't cover all the topics involved with being safe sexually. This chapter will help you find where to find the answers to the many, many questions you have about sexual safety.

There are three main search topics on sexual safety for teens. They are: safe sex tips for teens, safe dating tips for teens, and safe partying tips for teens. I like the ones that have simple and helpful lists and the ones that have indexes of every single topic you might want to explore. This is my take on what you need to know.

SAFE SEX

There are a lot of websites and books that are complete manuals on the basics of safe sexuality. I like the ones that are not just about safe sex, but about every question I have about my body, boys' bodies, my sexual body, sex, problems, itches, bumps, orgasms *and* safety tips.

* I found a book at a garage sale that I think is the best book out there on all aspects of sexuality. It has answered every question I've ever had. It is *Our Bodies, Ourselves.* You can download the entire book. There is a website you can browse. There are lots of others, but this is my favourite, but there are other Australian sites that are just as good.
* Find a few books or websites you like. There are usually good pamphlets at doctors' offices and health clinics. (Take them while you wait forever for the doctor.)
* It is clear from these resources that if you are going to be sexual, you cannot, I repeat cannot have sex without using condoms. Besides the obvious protection from becoming a teen parent, which I do think most of us don't want to become, we need protection from STDs. Some STDs can change your health forever. Some can end your life. Condoms are readily available at any supermarket or chemist.

* Some boys have a no condom rule. Since they will be having lots of babies and festering sores and transmittable gunk from other partners, I'd avoid these boys like the plague they can give you.
* Another vital part of sex safety is that we have to have a health professional we can go to and talk with. We need to be able to get questions answered. We need to be able to get birth control to go along with condoms. We need to be able to get help if we are worried about STDs or pregnancy. Some of us are comfortable talking with our doctors or nurse practitioners. Some feel more comfortable talking with someone at a health center that has a family planning clinic. These are usually free and private. You do not have to be over eighteen to go to them. It is often hard to go alone to these, so take a friend, a trusted adult, or better yet, your sexual partner.

DATING SAFELY

Again, just search *Safety tips for teen dating.* There are tons of great sites that give ideas about how to be alone with someone you are attracted to so you can get to know them better and maybe start down the bases, *and* be as safe as possible. Of course knowing how to say and hear '*No*' is vital. They have a million other ideas you might never come up with. Some of my favourites were:

* Go out, don't hang out. Going out to the movies or to eat is a better idea than going to someone's house and hanging out, especially when you are just getting to know them. Besides, getting out is fun.
* Know your limits and communicate them. We've gone over a lot of these, but I love this particular one: 'Communicate what makes you uncomfortable and what kinds of things you'd like to avoid on your date – whether it's sex, alcohol or spicy foods.'

PARTY SAFE

Parties are some of the least safe places for sexuality, but parties are all about sexuality. They are where we meet and flirt and celebrate and let loose. Some kids just don't go to parties because there is such a high risk for doing sexual things you may regret, but many take the risk because parties can be so fun.

The main reason regrettable sexual things happen at parties is because there are usually alcohol and drugs at these parties and it is hard to say no to them. In fact, it is normal to be so nervous when

So we get uninhibited and things happen. We make out with the guy who makes out with everyone. Someone grabs our hand and brings us to a secluded spot. Things happen quick. You don't want to make a scene by stopping unwanted sexual stuff – stuff that scares you.

Websites on safe dating for teens are amazing. They don't just tell you to avoid parties. They don't judge you. They give you a bag of tricks so that you can have fun and be safe. These are some of my favourites:

* Carry around a bottle of beer (or other drink) so that no-one keeps trying to get you to drink. You can also just put water in the bottle or in a cup.
* Always have a few trustworthy buddies who go to the party together, come home from the party together, and look out for each other.
* Eat and drink before you go to a party. (This helps you drink less.)
* Organise a time for your parents to pick you up.
* Have someone you can trust who can pick you up in an emergency. Hopefully this is your parents, but if not, choose another adult who will help.

One thing I would add to these safety tips is one of the most important factors that helps us be safe is to have conversations about sex with our parents.

ONE OF THE MOST IMPORTANT FACTORS THAT HELPS US BE SAFE IS TO HAVE CONVERSATIONS ABOUT SEX WITH OUR PARENTS.

I know some parents will freak out so much that it might not seem worth doing. But research shows that kids who can talk to their parents about sex are significantly safer than those who just try and do it on their own. You don't have to say, 'I'm thinking about having sex,' unless you have very cool parents – that probably will freak them out. But you can start by just asking them questions. You can ask them what they think about sex, what scares them, what advice they can give you. Even if the first few times you talk about sex it is awkward and they sort of freak out, if you keep talking to them it will become more comfortable and normal, which, in a perfect world, it should be!

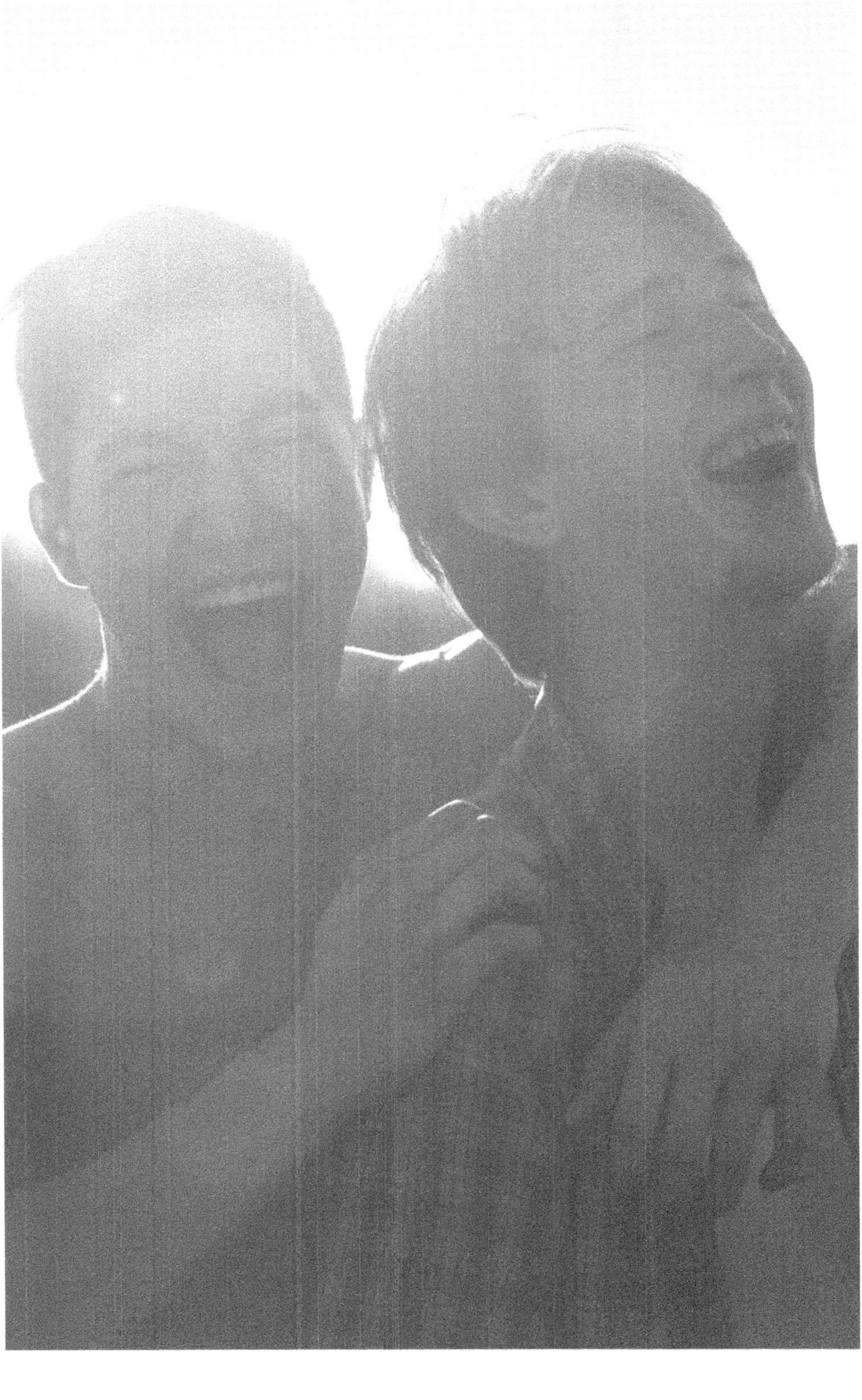

NINETEEN
SEXUAL ASSAULT

About one in five of us have been sexually assaulted in one form or another. Someone did something sexual to us that we did not agree to at a point in our lives. Regardless of how it happened, the experience can mess up your sex life if you don't heal up from it. It can make you afraid of sexuality. It can make you ashamed. It can make you disrespectful of your body and your sexuality. It can spark flashbacks as you become sexual. It can arouse sexual feelings in you that you didn't want to have.

That's the bad news.

The good news is that you can heal. The experience lasted minutes or hours of your entire life. It doesn't have to mess up you or your sex life forever. Without being flippant, millions of people have healed up from sex abuse, and have had sex lives that are just fine.

WITHOUT BEING FLIPPANT, MILLIONS OF PEOPLE HAVE HEALED UP FROM SEX ABUSE, AND HAVE HAD SEX LIVES THAT ARE JUST FINE.

First and foremost, you have to make sure it is not a secret. Tell someone. Tell anyone you trust. Let it out. Release it. The power the perpetrator tried to take from you is in the secret. Within the secret lies the guilt, shame, fear, blame and self-hatred.

Tell someone and get help.

Many teens are afraid to tell anyone about the abuse because they are afraid no-one will believe them, or that the perpetrator will hurt them, or that someone they love will go to jail, or worse, they will lose control again. Remember, you have all the control now. It is your body, your memory, your desire to heal and possibly, your desire to stop the perpetrator from harming others.

There are a lot of sites online for victims of sexual assault that can help until you are ready to talk to someone about it. Your future sexual happiness depends on you getting help from who you want, in your time, in your way.

YOUR FUTURE SEXUAL HAPPINESS DEPENDS ON YOU GETTING HELP FORM WHO YOU WANT, IN YOUR TIME, IN YOUR WAY.

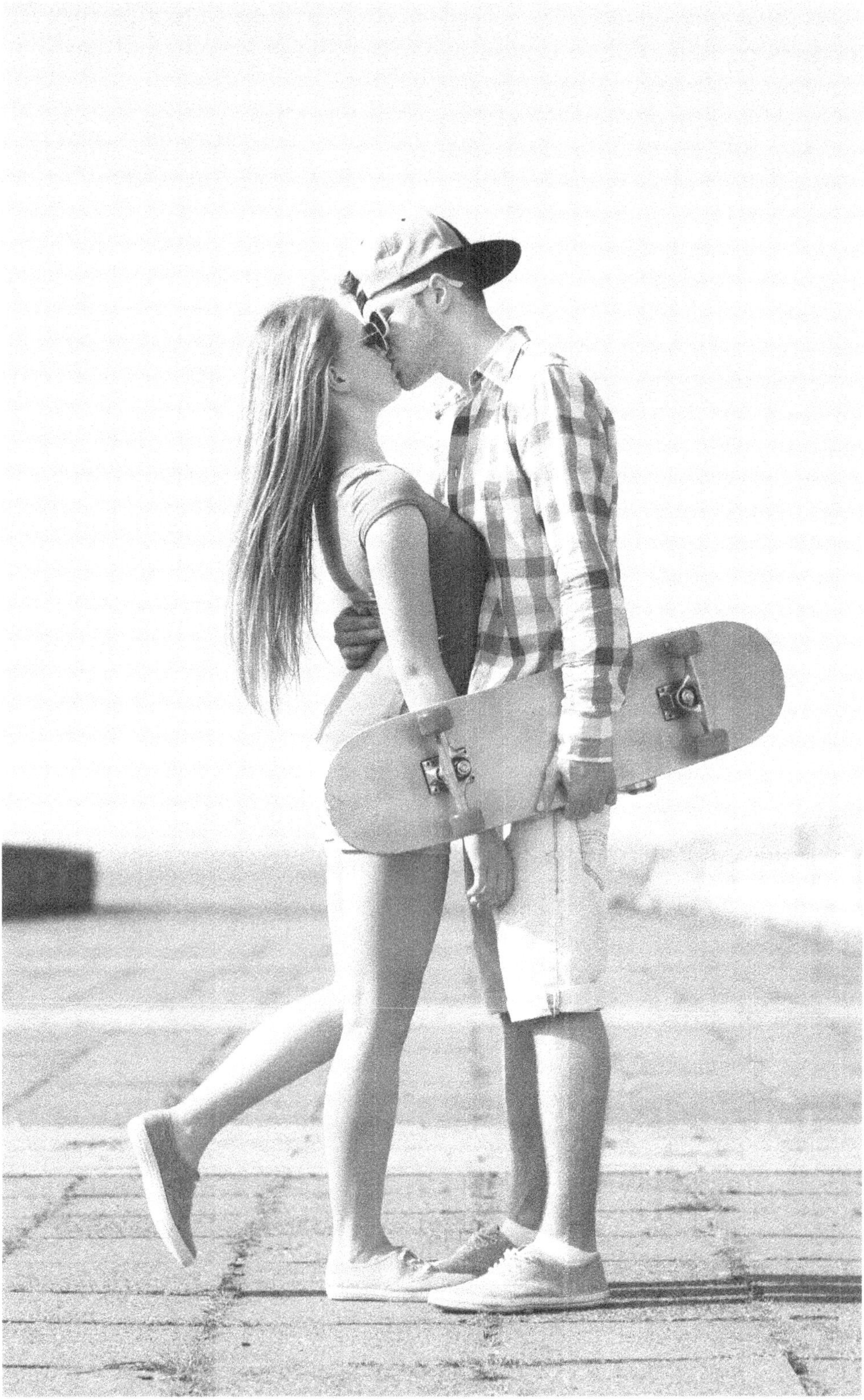

TWENTY
ACCEPT ONLY THE BEST, LADIES

Some boys are going to want to become sexual masters. They're going to learn to be great partners. They'll know how to flirt and hold hands and kiss softly. They'll know the bases and take their sweet time. They'll get to know you. They'll realise how amazing it is to connect with you. Some boys are going to become great lovers in their lifetime.

These are the ones we want. Wait for them. Insist upon these boys as boyfriends and lovers. Make these the popular boys.

We need to stop making the porn-educated boys as the guys everyone wants to date. Stop. That's all it takes. Cruel boys need to be shunned sexually and socially. They need to be ignored. They need to *not* get reinforced.

Why is the cruel boy, the player, still the model for popularity? These boys are mean. They steal our power. Yet we give them our attention, attraction and our bodies.

We are no longer Neanderthal chicks who need the strongest guys to hunt for meat. We are quite capable of taking ourselves to a nearby food shop. These guys scare us. They thrill us. They cross all the sexual lines. They go from, 'Hey, wassup?' to 'Are you a virgin?' (None of their business!) to 'Send me a nude' to 'Give me a hand job.'

They are notoriously bad at sex. Really. They don't even know this. They only know they want quick and frequent release. Do not be the vessel for some guy's quick release. He has a hand for that.

Just think:

* Is this what you really want? Insist on the very best for you and your body.
* Is the boy a jerk or is he great?
* How many girls has he hurt?
* How many girls has he had sex with? (This information is usually readily available.)
* How quickly did he go from 'Hi' to sexual talk and requests?
* How kind is he to others?
* How confused and pressured do you feel?
* How much do you think you can change him? (The more you think you can change him the less likely this guy is the one for you.)
* Does he know anything about sex as a sacred art?

THE MORE YOU THINK YOU CAN CHANGE HIM THE LESS LIKELY THIS GUY IS THE ONE FOR YOU.

I will also say this: a lot of boys are truly great, but have been miseducated about sex by porn. I wish this wasn't true. It isn't really up to girls to help these guys get on track, but I don't see too many great adults giving them the information. If you like a nice guy who seems to believe the porn rules, you might want to point him in the right direction to re-educate himself. See if he comes back around sexually smarter. Otherwise, get out of there.

We may just have to change the world one kiss at a time.

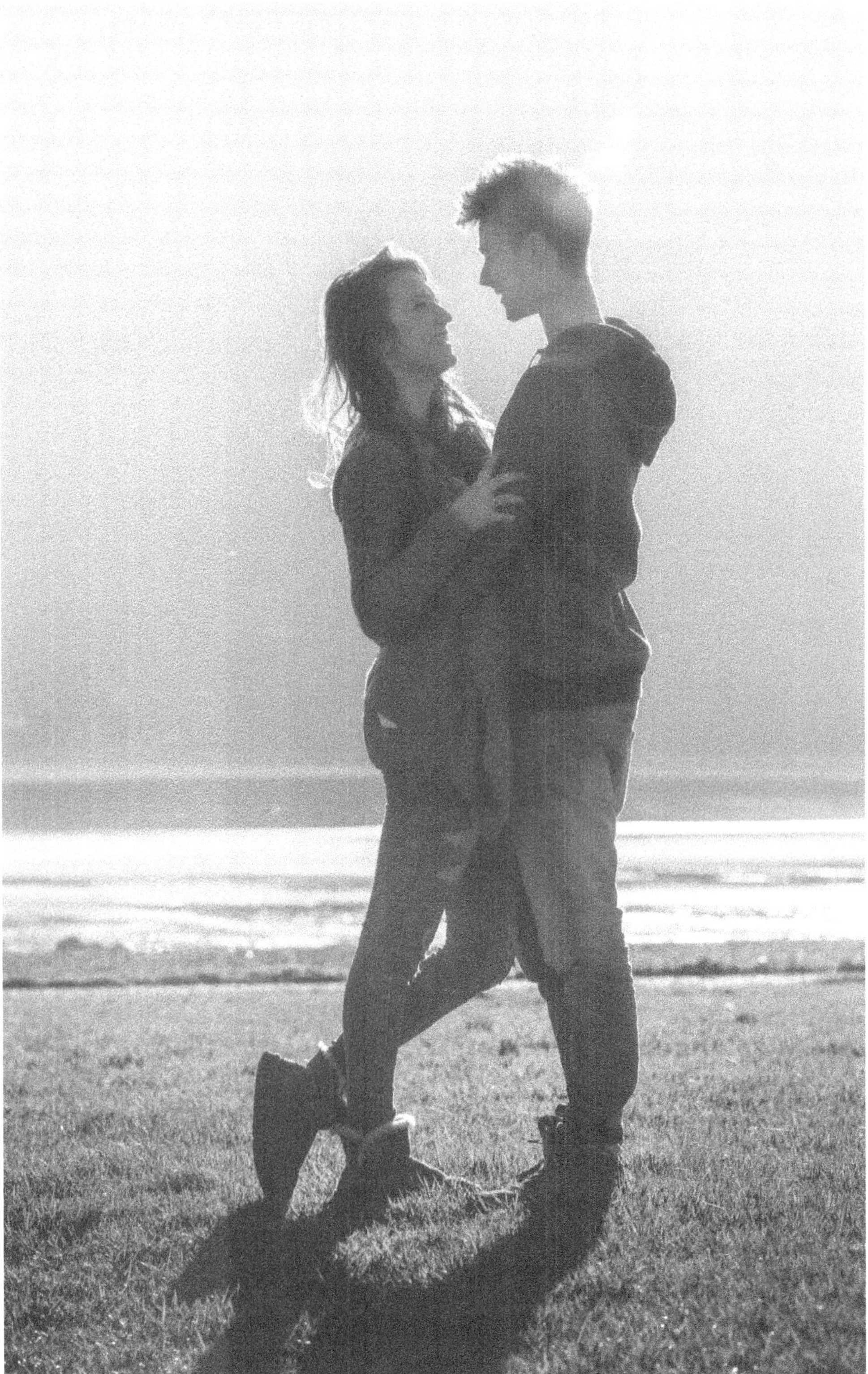

TWENTY-ONE
DUDES
BY JO SHA DUGAN

Hannah asked me to interview some guys and write this chapter. I just asked them one question:

What kind of man are you trying to be sexually?

Not very many of them answered the question directly... but here are some of the best things they said:

- ✹ I have no idea how to do this.
- ✹ I try, I really try to stay away from porn ... but at night ... when I can't sleep ...
- ✹ I really liked her.
- ✹ I hate when you are having fun and they get all weird ... clingy and shit.
- ✹ The thought of her with some other dude ... oh! It makes me crazy, and I hate being jealous.
- ✹ I think I hurt her. She's different.
- ✹ We sat in the bed of my truck. We were all wrapped up in each other. All we did was look at the stars all night. Everyone

else was partying inside. We didn't even kiss. It was the best night.
- I tried talking to my dad about sex and he took my phone away. Really … he took my phone away!
- I feel like I'm doing something wrong.
- I'm different when I'm online. I do things to girls no guy better ever do to my sister. I know … it's messed up.
- It's a game. Yeah (laughs), I lie about it all the time when I'm talking to guys. We're so full of shit when we're talking to each other.
- I get all 'See ya' after sex.
- I think she had a good time. I mean, I don't know if she did … I did … I never really thought about it.
- I want to be really good at this.
- We smiled when we kissed.

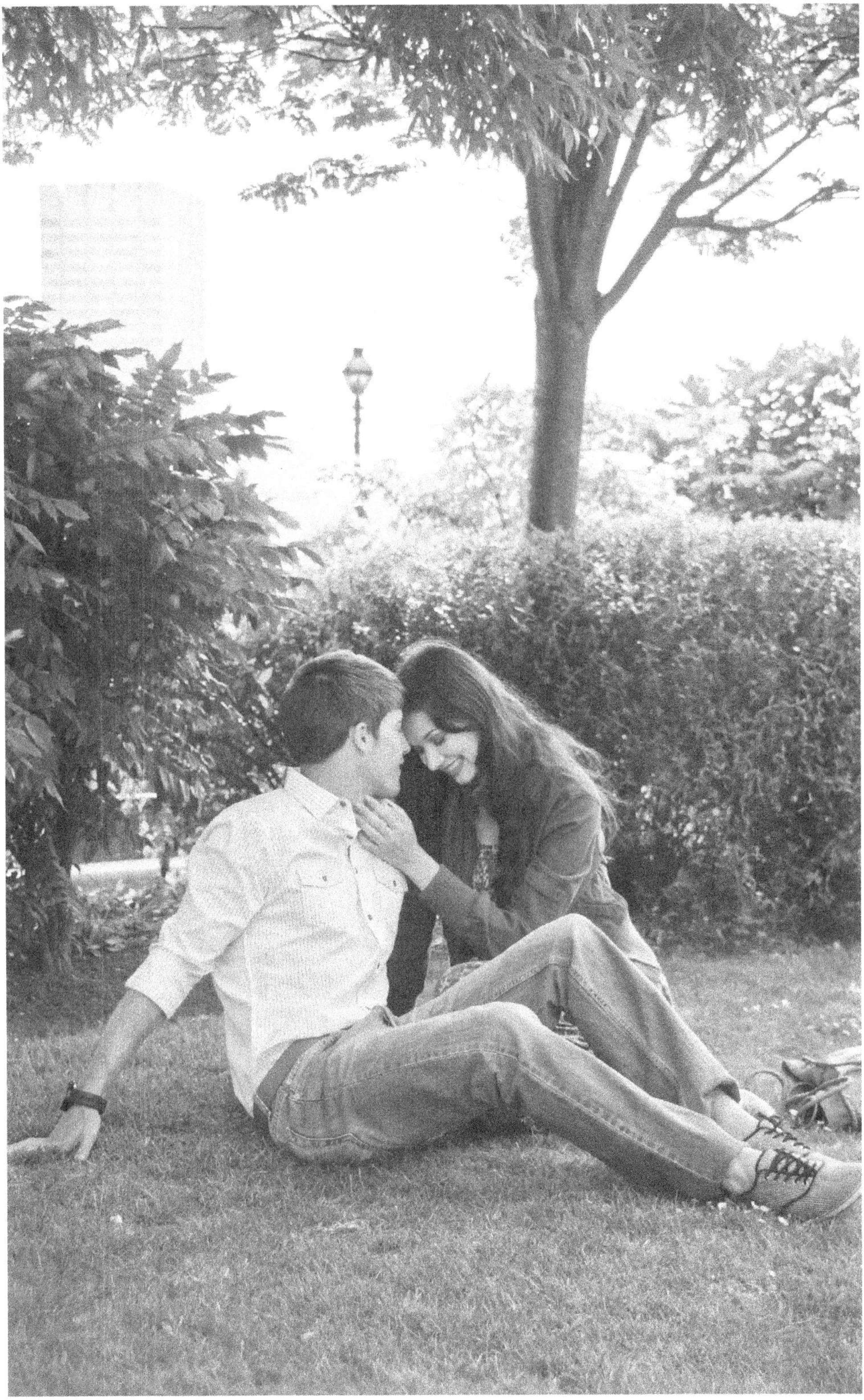

TWENTY-TWO
LET'S DO iT

I've said it before. It's time for a revolution, a sacred sexual revolution.

When I think of revolutions, I think of riots and anarchy and anger and flipped fingers. Yet the most successful revolutions come from an intense commitment of a large group of people to do something different from the well-established rules of society. So let's recap why we need a sexual revolution.

* We have bodies screaming for sexuality from about fifteen years of age.
* We have zero education on healthy, creative, playful, connecting sex.
* We have access to pornography and cyber-sexuality from a very young age.
* Many of us have been using the lies of porn as a model for real sex, especially the lie that we should be emotionally disconnected when we are being sexual.

- ✱ We are told to wait … and wait … and wait … possibly til marriage in our mid-twenties.
- ✱ We live in a culture that bombards us with sex, mostly to sell us stuff.
- ✱ A lot of us have been sexually abused.
- ✱ We are minimally supervised by the adults who make and enforce these rules.

In order to change our introduction to sex and our sexual futures we have to commit to ourselves, our sex lives, our future partners and our kids' sex lives. We just have to.

Change … that's the revolution. We need to do this together. We need to demand a lot from each other. Change our views on self-pleasure. Stay away from porn, or at least don't use it as a model for sex. Explore sacred sex texts. Be mindful. Demand sexually mindful partners. Heal up from sex abuse. Go slow. Learn and practice.

Let's become sexual masters.

Let's save the world through great connections.

POSTSCRIPT

I am very glad you read this book.

I wrote it when my teenage daughter asked me to tell her everything I wanted her to know about sex ... in *written* form.

As a therapist who's been talking to teens about sexuality forever, I had plenty to say. Because even though bodies and hearts work the same way they've always worked, there are significant differences between the way you, who grew up connected to the internet, and we who did not, entered into our sexual lives.

The main difference between your generation's sexuality and mine is that, more than likely, your first visuals of sexuality were online, you were probably young, they were probably explicit, and they probably modelled emotional disconnection.

This has effected what I call the *moment*.

The *moment* happens when people who are attracted to each another, who may have shared a sweet flirt, held hands or gazed into each other's eyes, just at that moment, silently decide to go further in touching... lips, bodies, perhaps everything.

In the old days, at the moment we decided to become more intimate with our bodies, we also became more intimate with our emotional connections. We drew emotionally closer to them. We were very aware of their tremendous worth. Our hearts and bodies worked in tandem.

But the models you and/or your potential partners have been exposed to from the beginning of your sexual lives taught you the opposite response to the *moment*. You've been taught to disconnect emotionally just as your bodies are beginning to become intimate.

It's as if you call someone you adore, and right as you are going to tell them how you feel ... you hang up the phone. I mean you might keep talking ... you might say everything you wanted to say, but who cares...you hung up. They won't hear you.

Big deal or not?

What might be the impact on your life if, during your most intimate physical act, the habit is to disconnect emotionally from the person you are being intimate with? I think it makes it easier to disconnect with and discount the worth of others in all areas of our lives, not just sexually. Perhaps the increase in teen bullying, cyber-cruelty, lack of focus, depression and anxiety are direct consequences of this.

The very good news is that you are brilliant ... you really want to love and be loved ... you adore sexy romance. All it really takes to get back the *moment* is to know the difference between emotionally connected and disconnected sexuality. Then you can accept only the best for yourself and others.

That's it.

I believe you can change the world one great kiss at a time.

ELIZABETH CLARK

STEVE BIDDULPH'S
RAISING GIRLS

From babyhood to womanhood – helping your daughter to grow up wise, warm and strong

Author of million copy bestseller Raising Boys

Steve Biddulph's Raising Girls

ISBN: 9781921462351

Steve Biddulph's Raising Boys
ISBN:9781921462863

STEVE BIDDULPH

The New Manhood

20TH ANNIVERSARY EDITION

'Read this book and you'll make the world a better place, by making yourself a better man.'
RICHARD GLOVER, ABC BROADCASTER, AUTHOR OF *THE MUD HOUSE*

The most influential book on men's lives

The New Manhood
ISBN:9780987419699